I Can Do That!

Advice for Spiritual Entrepreneurs

By Walter F. Johnson III

Published by
Evening Post Books
Charleston, South Carolina

Copyright © 2010 by Walter F. Johnson III
All rights reserved.
First edition

Editors: John M. Burbage, Jason Lesley
Designer: Gill Guerry

First printing 2010
Printed in the United States of America

A CIP catalog record for this book has been applied
for from the Library of Congress.

ISBN: 978-0-9825154-3-3

To Doris,

my long-time friend and

childhood sweetheart, my lover, my soul mate,

my wife and mother of our six children

and grandmother of our fourteen

grandchildren.

I Can Do That!

Advice for Spiritual Entrepreneurs

By Walter F. Johnson III

Evening Post Publishing Co.
Charleston, South Carolina

Foreword

Wally Johnson chuckles as he listens to a so-called self-made multi-millionaire on television brag about how he got rich quick. "He's way too proud of himself," Johnson notes with a grin. "That's the kind of pride that makes the top-seven list of deadly sins — the kind that will kill you spiritually."

Johnson is a religious man. He was raised Episcopalian in Charleston, S.C., and converted to Catholicism while in college in West Virginia. He attends mass at least three times a week. He prays to the Father, the Son, the Holy Spirit, the Mother of Jesus Mary Ever Virgin, the Apostles and other saints and martyrs. He doesn't discuss his faith often, but he does describe himself as a "spiritual entrepreneur."

"Listen to that guy," he says about the pitchman on the TV screen. "He rambles about self-assurance and self-determination and self-discipline and self-reliance and so on and so forth. People actually believe that 99.9 percent of entrepreneurial success is self-generated. They are so self-focused, so predictable and so wrong. They're missing the most important part of the ultimate business plan.

"When creditors are lined up outside your door and paying customers are nowhere to be found, the soundest strategy for success is to drop down on your knees and pray for guidance. It works for me but not always at the precise moment I ask or exactly as I expect. However, the Lord is always there for me. Like the old Negro spiritual says, He's an On-Time God."

Walter F. Johnson III knows what he's talking about. The 70-year-old African American who spent the first ten years of his life in the Gadsden-

Green public housing projects on the west side of Charleston, radiates self-esteem. He sold Post-Courier newspapers as a child, excelled in sports, graduated from high school and college, joined the United States Army and became a medical platoon leader in the 82nd Airborne Division, served in Korea and Vietnam, earned the equivalent of two master's degrees while in the military, was chief of the Army's Medical Service Corps and directed the U.S. Army Medical Department's worldwide health services operations, rose to the rank of brigadier general, took a civilian job with the American Hospital Association, started an international contracting company that generated more than $150 million in revenues annually, sold it to Lockheed Martin Corporation and wrote a book about it.

I Can Do That! — Advice for Spiritual Entrepreneurs is not a success story about a black kid who grew up "in the projects" of the segregated South. It's a collection of success stories about Wally Johnson, starting in 1952 when he was 13 years old and delivering newspapers across town.

"Realizing that more money could be made with a larger route, I quickly applied for and got bigger ones for both the morning and afternoon papers," he explains. "I entered a subscription-sales contest with the intention of winning. I came in second. My father and I attended a luncheon in honor of the local carriers and got a free harbor tour of Fort Sumter — the place where the Civil War began. Imagine that! My picture ran on the front page the next day along with the other winners — all of them white except me."

That Sunday in the sanctuary of Calvary Episcopal Church on Line Street where Wally was an altar boy, the minister praised his accomplishment, noting that he was the only "colored" kid in the photograph.

"I was standing up front, facing the congregation when the preacher said it. I saw the pleased looks on my parents' faces. I got my first taste of success and I liked it and I've been driven to succeed ever since."

He hired help for his budding newspaper business, sent out the bills, collected the cash, paid the expenses, kept the records, made money. By the time he graduated from Immaculate Conception High School on Coming Street, he had the largest newspaper route in the city. Three decades later, he was nominated by Post-Courier Editor Thomas R. Waring to the International Newspaper Carriers Hall of Fame and received the Association of Circulation Managers' Golden Medallion.

"I still think I should have come in first instead of second in that new-subscriber contest," Johnson adds. And he's not kidding.

Growing up black in the 1940s and 1950s in Charleston was an extraordinary challenge. But Wally Johnson overcame the cultural, social and political divide. Despite the obstacles, he took advantage of America's democratic spirit — that peculiar attitude that the United States is one nation, under God, where each citizen is at least as good as anyone else. That spirit is what fuels the entrepreneurial self-confidence that drives Wally Johnson today. He was inspired from the start by his family, friends and teachers. And with a lot of help from that curious notion most of us recognize as the Almighty, he took advantage of America's democratic spirit time after time.

I Can Do That! — Advice for Spiritual Entrepreneurs, by Walter F. Johnson III, is a most unusual "self-help book," the first offered by the Evening Post Publishing Company. I hope you enjoy it as much as we have enjoyed working with this remarkable man who knows success and is happy to share all he has learned to achieve it.

John M. Burbage, Editor
Charleston, S.C.
EveningPostBooks.com

Acknowledgements

"Son, give credit where credit is due," my father, Walter F. Johnson Jr., often said when I was growing up in Charleston, S.C. So thanks, Dad. I could not have done it without your guidance. I know you are pleased with your only son. I wish you were here now to enjoy our success.

My father was a butler, handyman, mail carrier, insurance agent, civic leader, Freemason and entrepreneur. He was one of several people who inspired me since the day I was born in 1939.

My mother was another. She was a domestic servant who also worked part time at the local cigar factory and at a wholesale supplies store. But she was always there when I got home from school. I was an only child and she spoiled me, knowing that my father would apply the proper amount of discipline at precisely the right moment to prevent his son from curdling.

My parents instilled in me essential values that, unfortunately, too many children are not getting today for a variety of reasons. My parents also gave me love — the kind that is pure and never vacillates. I'm thankful for that. It is my hope that this book will inspire young people to set their goals high and work hard to reach them regardless of disadvantages.

I am indebted to my teachers at Immaculate Conception Catholic School who nurtured and bolstered my budding self-esteem. It was through them, too, that I realized early that ambitious dreams could come true, especially if the dreamer is open, honest, focused and willing to work for it.

My Uncle Gilbert Johnson's wise counsel and sound advice continue to steady me. I'm also grateful Aunt Audrey insisted on being my second mother back in the early years. Having one mom who genuinely cared was grand. Having two was magnificent.

Throughout my life as a student, athlete, parent, U.S. Army officer, hospital association director and owner of Eagle Group International Inc., I've been blessed with vigorous, fun-loving friends who have enriched my life incalculably. They are numerous and I'm hesitant to try and list them all here because I might leave someone out. They know who they are. Thanks to all, especially my Eagle Group family.

Many people with whom I have associated in the business world have helped me as well. Even the detractors and the second-guessers and the dirty dealers deserve some of the credit for my accomplishments because they kept me attentive and resolute during difficult times.

I am especially fortunate to have a wise and beautiful wife. Doris Wright Johnson has been my loving partner and trusted confidant for more than fifty-seven years. I could not have done it without her.

And thank Goodness, too, for all six of our children and their spouses; and for our 14 grandchildren, at least two of them who surely will become U.S. presidents some day. Their "Poppy" hopes this book inspires them to read, to think, to dream, to pray and to work hard to achieve their objectives.

I am especially grateful to God Almighty for granting me so many blessings. Without God, I am nothing.

Thank you Lord for the strength to withstand so many setbacks. Thank you for allowing our enterprise to prosper. Thank you for providing me clarity to recognize sound business principles and for endowing me with the discipline to apply them consistently.

Your devoted servant,

Wally.

Chapter 1

"God, have I lost my mind? Am I about to go chasing after something that's not a part of the big plan?"

My name is Wally Johnson and I pray a lot. I always have — every day and every night — and God listens. He always has and always will. So again, as usual, I open my eyes slowly, looking around for a clue, a sign of divine intervention. But the only thing I see is the wood-paneled study of my home in Georgetown, S.C., looking exactly as it did five minutes ago.

"Darn!"

I laugh easily, still looking around. Was a burning bush supposed to light up the place? The paneling in my study glows warmly as spring sunshine streams through the windows, glistens off the rows of plaques and trophies and other mementos collected through the years. I'm 56 years old in the spring of 1995 and already retired as a brigadier general in the United States Army. I'm working as a civilian health services executive making more than $200,000 a year. I own homes in Atlanta and South Carolina and a 37-foot-cabin cruiser. I have no financial worries. None!

So why am I asking God for help on a hunch that requires we risk everything and start a business? Perhaps divine intervention isn't what I need. Psychiatric help is more like it.

It's taken me a long time to figure out what I want to be when I grow up. At an age when sane people are preparing for retirement, I'm about to start a business, a risky one at that. I'm about to try and take advantage of my expertise in the medical service and administration field and become a contracting consultant. I'm looking up at my own Mount Everest and I'm going to use every ounce of my energy to climb it. Even though I've never owned a business other than a childhood newspaper route, I know I can reach the summit. It's a spiritual thing, a matter of the soul. I thrive on challenges. I'm an over-achiever. I often tell myself and all who listen, "I can do that!"

I leave the study and head to the bedroom. Doris is in there reading the newspaper, drinking her morning coffee. I rehearse the reasons why I'm going to suggest that we risk everything on this entrepreneur thing. I need something more powerful, more persuasive than, "Trust me, Honey. It just feels right."

I've always brought home the paycheck while Doris has managed the household, which included six demanding children. But we are a team. No sense in my acting like an Army general now. She won't allow it.

I walk into the bedroom and clear my throat. She lowers the newspaper and stares with a quizzical smile. She's still my beautiful Doris.

I met her when we were teenagers in Charleston. I went to Immaculate Conception, the only all-black Catholic high school in South Carolina. She went to Avery Institute and later to Burke, an all-black public high school in the city. I was a star of the football and basketball teams. She was a drum majorette of the high-stepping Bulldog marching band. I've always loved that girl.

"Good morning again," I hear myself saying as I give Doris a quick kiss.

Her eyebrows rise. "What's on your mind?" she asks.

Whenever I have anything important to accomplish, I do not procrastinate and this time is no exception.

"We've been blessed with health, children, grandchildren and financial security," I say confidently, "but we can do better."

Doris folds the paper and listens. Her eyes never leave mine. When

13

I was an Army officer, I addressed entire battalions of soldiers. I've also briefed the U.S. Joint Chiefs of Staff. I am good at expressing myself. I proceed with my presentation to my wife, expecting to hear, "Have you gone crazy?"

She listens carefully as I tick off the reasons why we should risk all of our earthly possessions to start a business of our own. I don't dwell on the negatives.

Doris continues to look into my eyes and says, "Well, Walter, this is a surprise, but you did tell me back when we were dating that you would become a millionaire, and the last time I checked our bank statement, you haven't made it yet."

At that moment, a shock of energy electrifies the Johnson household. Doris and I discuss plans for the new company. I understand the medical service field, and the opportunity to get into the contract consulting business with the federal government is available to minorities such as myself. I have been involved with administering medical-services projects practically all my life, and since I admire eagles and all the bird stands for, the nation's stunning symbol will be part of our new company's name.

Later that morning back in my study, I'm as euphoric as a child at Christmas, but it doesn't take long for my optimism to fade. But that's OK. If you're going to ditch a $200K-per-year job to start a business on a hunch and you don't feel somewhat nervous, you're not normal. I felt the same way about people who claimed to feel no fear seconds before jumping out of an aircraft while in flight at 12,000 feet. That was before I earned my jump wings as an officer in the 82nd Airborne Division.

Fear. Paranoia. Anticipation. Excitement. I'm feeling all four as I prepare Eagle Group International Inc. for takeoff. Of course, financial ruin is a concern, but I've been broke before. I can live with that.

Will I succeed? Only one way to find out.

Jesus, I don't know jack about running a business! Please prop me up in my leaning places because I'm about to take a running leap. I continue to be grateful for your love and blessings.

Your humble servant again,
Wally

Chapter 2

Twenty-seven years is a long time in a single line of work. That's how long I proudly served in the United States Army.

Soon after my promotion to brigadier general, I tried on my general officer blue uniform and stood looking in our full-length mirror admiring the bright braids on the jacket sleeves. That's when Doris walked into the room and asked what I was doing.

"Just wondering," I said, still looking at myself in the mirror.

"About what?"

"I'm wondering how many great generals there have been in the history of the United States Army — men like George Washington, Pershing, Patton and Eisenhower."

Doris glanced back at me and said, "I don't know how many great generals there have been, but I do know there is one less than you think."

Three years later, in 1988, I hung up my uniform in my closet and left it there. I had achieved the rank of brigadier general and was the chief of the U.S. Army's Medical Service Corps. I was responsible for training, management and career development of more than 5,000 Medical Service Corps officers arrayed into thirty-plus specialties, including audiology, psychology, optometry, podiatry, aero-medical evacuation, research biochemistry and health services administration to name a few.

I was not a medical doctor. I majored in zoology at West Virginia State College. I was the youngest officer, the first non-physician and the first African American to direct the Army Medical Department's health-services operations. Unfortunately, brigadier general (one star) was the highest rank authorized for my position. I could go no higher. That's frustrating for someone like me. So after serving three years as a brigadier general, I requested retirement from the military at the age of 49.

My last duty station was the Office of the United States Army Surgeon General in Alexandria, Va. My family and I lived in Woodbridge, twenty-two miles south of Washington, D.C. I carpooled at that time with Walter Berry, a six-foot-six African-American colonel I'd known for years. We were headed to work one morning when Walt suggested that I'd be a great business owner in the civilian world.

"Think about it, Wally," he said, and I laughed. Forty-five minutes later we parked the car where we worked. I remember telling him that I appreciated having a paycheck automatically deposited in my bank account every two weeks, adding, "I have NO desire to get away from that. Absolutely none."

"Just a suggestion, Wally," he said. "When you work for someone else, there's a limit on what you can make. You know that as well as I do, and it is frustrating."

I always admired people who owned their own businesses. My father owned a music shop and vending machines at one time long ago. I can close my eyes now and see him in my mind. He was a handsome man.

He wore black horn-rim glasses. He was born in 1917 in Charleston and graduated from Avery High School on Bull Street. He worked as a butler and handyman for U.S. District Judge J. Waties Waring. My father spoke highly of Judge Waring, who asked my father for advice about lots of things. My father often spoke fondly of their relationship and his help.

J. Waties Waring was a white, eighth-generation Charlestonian of high social standing who was the first federal jurist in the nation to declare that "separate-but-equal" public schools were not equal at all. The judge was in his 60s when he left his long-time, very traditional wife of

Charleston and married a liberal woman from the North. The so-called "blue-bloods" of downtown Charleston were mortified. The divorce and his surprise support for civil rights was big news locally.

The judge and his new wife entertained African Americans inside their home on Meeting Street. Some say the Ku Klux Klan organized demonstrations in front of the house during which a cross was burned and someone threw a brick with a racial threat on it through a window while the Warings and guests were dining. But Judge Waring did not capitulate.

His dissent was in support of Briggs versus Elliott, which originated in Clarendon County, S.C. It was launched in 1950 and led by NAACP attorney Thurgood Marshall, who later became a U.S. Supreme Court justice. Judge Waring's position formed the legal foundation for the landmark Brown versus Board of Education case, which led to desegregation of public schools in the United States.

Judge Waring also ordered S.C. Democratic Party officials to open their rolls to all qualified voters without regard to their race, and that equal pay must be guaranteed for otherwise equally qualified public school teachers.

My father married my mother when they were teenagers. Both his parents died, so he and my mother took in his younger sister and two younger brothers. They were children when I was born. For the first ten years of my life, all six of us lived in a two-bedroom, one-bathroom public-housing apartment not far from the white-males-only Citadel military college.

I shared a bedroom with my parents. They were teenagers when they took on the responsibility of raising four children, and they did it well. Family members and friends volunteered to take in my father's sister and brothers. But he did not want his siblings to be split up. I suspect he had made a promise to his dying mother that he would keep the family together.

My mother was a beautiful woman. I remember as a pre-teen going to a basketball game in which my father was playing. I was sitting in the stands with a group of older boys who were in high school.

When Mom walked into the gymnasium, one of the older boys asked, "Who is that fox?" The comments like that continued. But I said nothing. My young friends knew who she was, but they didn't say anything either, thank Goodness.

When I arrived home after the game, Mom asked why I didn't come and sit beside her. I did not answer that one. I quickly left the room.

Although those early years were tough, they were filled with fun and laughter. We were poor but we never felt that way. Except for an automobile, I thought we had everything. My father had a driver's license and I knew it. I saw him driving a U.S. government mail truck at times. But he mostly traversed the city on a bicycle while the rest of us either walked or rode the bus.

It was a big deal when my father came home one day and announced we were going to move three blocks away to a two-bedroom house. By then my aunt and uncles were old enough to take care of themselves. Our new house on Spring near President streets was in a mixed-race neighborhood. That was not unusual in many sections of Charleston. A Jewish family lived on one side of our house and a Greek family who ran a corner store was on the other side.

Charleston is an historic port city. People of various races and cultures have been living and working there since Colonial times. It's a cosmopolitan city, too. Always has been because of the shipping trade. But most of my friends were African Americans who lived nearby in the projects. That's where I spent most of my time when I was not in school. I played football, basketball, baseball and ran track. Most of the black kids played sports. There was not much else to do back then. Nobody had money.

We knew our neighbors in public housing projects. If you were a stranger to the neighborhood, especially after dark, you could be in trouble. The projects were filled with young alpha males, including me, eager to prove themselves.

But extreme violence was rare. It was usually a lot of jive talking but there were no guns — a knife, occasionally, but no firearms.

Success in anything starts at home with parents who care about their children. My passion for hard work is a direct result of seeing my father work two jobs almost all of his life. He was often critical of people who did not work or could not hold a steady job.

I cannot adequately express his disdain of those who could work but did not. No telling what he would think about the situation today. I had no doubt in my mind back then that to achieve anything in life, one must be willing to work for it. Success is directly related to a desire to work.

That's what the term "Moving On Up" is about. Most African Americans are familiar with the television program about the Jefferson family whose theme song is about moving up the socio-economic ladder in America. The Johnson family was like that. My father often spoke about what it takes to make it to a higher level, and he made sure I was listening.

He emphasized that I would not move up in life if I waited for someone to give me instructions. "Take the initiative," he said, "and work hard to be the best that you can."

I recall a conversation I had with a military friend soon after I became a brigadier general. I told him that I planned to retire a year earlier than I had to.

"Why, Wally?" he asked.

I said I was looking toward the future; that I wanted to continue to "move on up."

"You're too ambitious," he replied. "Retire and stay on cruise control for the rest of your life. That's what I intend to do. We've earned it."

Jesus, Thank you for the opportunity to grow up in a public housing project and learn the lessons of life.

Your constant student,

Wally

Chapter 3

When I joined the military in 1961, I had every intention to work after I retired from active service. While laziness had nothing to do with my desire to continue to work, a lot of people back then assumed most African Americans were lazy, even those who were military officers.

When I was a second lieutenant in the 82nd Airborne Division, I had a supervisor who assumed that I was not as motivated as my white colleagues. He enjoyed embarrassing me in public by insinuating I either lacked the knowledge or was too lazy to do my job. His attitude was bolstered by the fact that he held a higher rank.

For example, when our unit at Fort Bragg, N.C., underwent annual general inspection, the division's inspector general singled out my medical platoon as the best in the company. Yet, the next day we were the only platoon that did not get holiday leave. So, I asked the battle group executive officer (my supervisor's superior) if he thought it was ironic that our platoon — cited as the best — was not given permission to take off like all the rest.

"Indeed, your platoon was best prepared for annual inspection," the executive officer told me, "and it deserves to have time off. Please tell them they may take leave as well."

I eventually proved something to that condescending supervisor who enjoyed putting me down. Twelve years later, not long after I graduated from the Army's Command and General Staff College — a one-year course for outstanding officers — I ran into this man at the commissary (grocery store) at Fort Leavenworth, Kan.

"Wally," he said. "What are you doing here? Are you a medic at the base hospital?"

"No," I responded, adding, "Are you attending Command and General Staff College (C&GSC)?"

I waited for one of his typical sarcastic comments, and he did not disappoint me.

"Yes," he said, "But why are you here?"

I explained to him that I graduated from Command and General Staff College the previous year, and did so well that I was selected to go on to graduate school. "I am here because I am attending the University of Missouri at Kansas City. When will you be going to graduate school?"

My parents did not go to college, but I did. While at West Virginia State, I married Doris, enjoyed an active social life, had two children, studied hard and took four years of Reserved Officers Training Corps courses. Upon graduation, I joined the U.S. Army as a second lieutenant.

The Army was good for me. I learned discipline. It was an ordered world. The military was also good to me. Four of my six children were born, free of charge, in military hospitals. We bought food and other necessities at low prices in commissaries and post exchanges. Upon retirement, I was paid two-thirds of my $86,000 active duty salary annually plus benefits. We were comfortable and secure.

After my retirement from the Army, I was nervous about my transition to civilian life. But whenever those feelings came, I asked God for advice and assurance, and sure enough, the bubbles of anxiety soon burst and I'd move on up with determination and confidence. God was always there for me.

Upon retirement from the military, I immediately took a job with the American Hospital Association and we moved to Dallas where I became a regional director for member hospitals in Texas, Oklahoma, Louisiana and Arkansas. The pay was about the same as what I was making in the Army, so my income essentially doubled. The checks continued to go directly into my bank account.

The first day of my new job with the hospital association was Oct. 1, 1988, and I quickly adjusted to the challenge. I made it clear from the start that I was not interested initially in filling one of three senior executive jobs that were open in the organization. My immediate goal was to begin as a field representative, so I took one of the regional director positions. I planned to work harder and smarter than everyone else and prove that I was not just another retired military officer looking for a cushy civilian job. I also wanted to show that I could work with all kinds of people regardless of their race and upbringing.

The person who held the regional directorship prior to my getting the job happened to be a Catholic nun who had been a school principal and later the chief executive officer of a small hospital. The first public appearance I made in my new job was at a regional meeting in Fort Worth. When I stepped to the podium and looked out over the audience, I did not see a single black person out there, and I was certain all who were listening that day were wondering how I would do compared to my predecessor.

"Hello everyone," I said. "My name is Wally Johnson and for those who are looking for the Sister, I want you to know that she has retired. I also ask you not to look upon this situation as if you are losing your Sister but rather look at it as if you are gaining a Brother," which certainly broke the ice with that crowd.

I had a three-person staff and did a lot of traveling to various hospitals in the four-state region. And I made it clear to my staff and everyone else I met that I did not want to be called "Gen. Johnson." I told them "Wally" was my name and that I liked it very much. We had almost

2,000 hospitals in our region and my objective was to visit all of them, signing up as many non-members into the association that we could.

To maximize visits and simultaneously cut travel expenses, I usually traveled by car. I'd drive throughout the region, stopping in as many hospitals as possible along the way. And sure enough, the AHA membership grew rapidly. Each month, we visited more hospitals monthly and signed up more non-members than our counterparts did in all the other regions combined

At one meeting in Louisiana, the state hospital association president asked me where I was staying that night. I said I was staying at such-and-such motel, not far away, and that I had gotten a very good rate.

He was shocked, saying, "I would never stay that in that place overnight and I am white … they have a lot of racism there."

The other regional directors in the association soon joked in a friendly way about my approach to doing my work. "You're taking a great job and turning it into real work," one of them said.

Eventually, I did get a call from the AHA president asking if I was interested in becoming a senior vice president and working out of the Chicago headquarters. That was on a Thursday. I reported for duty in the Windy City the following Monday.

During my tenure as senior vice president, I witnessed massive changes in both structure of the organization and personnel. I traveled throughout the United States, regularly visiting association executives in more than 75 offices. After almost two years in Chicago, I decided it was time to move on, so I submitted my resignation.

The president at that time told me he did not want me to leave and asked if I was interested in leading an effort to recruit more minorities and women into senior health-services jobs. Soon I was heading up the establishment of the Institute for Diversity in Health Services Administration, headquartered in Atlanta, Ga. It was a collaborative effort under the auspices of the American Hospital Association, the American College of Health Services Administration and the National Association of Health Services Administration.

We sponsored a summer intern program for college students, the issuance of grants for tuition assistance and other financial aide, established a resident program and other educational projects.

Working successfully within any bureaucracy requires patience and knowledge of how to make the system work for you. I always tried to first understand the organization's culture before I took initiatives. This is the approach I used when I joined the American Hospital Association. I never considered myself to be aggressive in my relationships with anyone in the organization. Diplomacy was important at all times.

And I certainly did not want to rely on my reputation for previous successes. I earned the respect of my supervisors as well as my subordinates.

I recall that it was also during my stint with the American Health Association that my dear friend Walt Berry called. He, too, had retired from the military and gotten a civilian job. He was a consultant who contracted projects through the U.S. Department of Defense.

Contracting consultants provide services, supplies and equipment, conduct studies, give advice and counsel on a variety of administrative, logistical, technical and other matters required by government officials. In almost all cases, consultants solve problems and provide for a more efficient use of resources.

"This consulting stuff is easy, Wally," he said. "You can do it in your sleep. You should start a contract-consulting firm in the area of health services."

"It's a little late in the game for this old dog," I responded. We talked a bit longer and I thanked him and hung up.

About a year later, I was at a luncheon along with Army Surgeon General Sid LaNoue, who I knew well. In the course of making his rounds, he came to my table and sat down. "So Wally, how's soft civilian life agreeing with you?" he asked with a half-smile.

I bring out the jovial side of people because I'm that way myself. But Sid wasn't making small talk. He wanted to know if I would help him by starting a company focused on solving U.S. Defense Department health-services problems.

"Go out on a limb like that at this point in my life, Sid? Nooooo, I don't think so!" I said with a laugh. Taking on the risk and aggravation of becoming an entrepreneur made no sense to me at that time in my life. What would be the point?

A few months later, I was in my office when the phone rang. It was Ernest Freeman, a retired Army sergeant major and friend. He worked for a Department of Defense consulting firm. He said a health-services consulting contract was coming up and I'd be the perfect person to reel it in.

Now, I've never said I was the brightest bulb in the stadium. But a light flickered over my head. I told Ernest that I would consider it. "Will you put some money into this consulting business if I do?" I asked. He declined.

His response made no difference by then. The light over my head burned brightly. Starting a defense contracting consulting firm might work, I told myself.

It had been seven years since I left the Army and I was earning in excess of $200,000 annually as a senior vice president with the American Hospital Association. I had also helped establish the Institute of Diversity in Atlanta to help minorities and women land executive jobs in the burgeoning health-service industry.

But I was not satisfied. I was 56 years old and keenly aware that I was closer to the end of my life than the beginning. It was also clear to me that I didn't have enough money to adequately capitalize such a venture.

So I did what I always do when I need help. I got down on my knees and prayed, and before I knew exactly what had transpired, I walked away from my six-figure job into the uncertain world of entrepreneurship.

Eagle Group International Inc. took flight in March 1995. Atlanta was home base because it was the closest major city to Georgetown, S.C., where Doris and I lived in a beautiful, two-story home in a great neighborhood called, of all things, Wedgefield Plantation.

But sadly, Walt Berry died in a car crash shortly before Eagle Group got off the ground.

Lord, I praise and thank you for your guidance. Please bless the work of my head and my hands on this day you have made. Keep me humble in victory. Grant me the maturity and patience to accept setbacks as learning experiences. Give me strength to move on. Amen.

Your Reluctant Entrepreneur,

Wally

Chapter 4

I didn't suddenly start communicating with God when I formed Eagle Group International. I've pestered Him my entire life. I got clued in to the power of prayer as a boy in South Carolina.

My third-grade teacher at Immaculate Conception Catholic School organized a raffle where the prize was a beautiful silver necklace that I wanted for my mother, Inez Johnson. One of Mama's favorite sayings was, "God answers the prayers of children," and I decided to prove it.

So Walter Jr. and Inez Johnson's only child prayed morning, noon and night to win that necklace. On the day the winner was to be announced, I flew out of bed two hours earlier than usual. Sometimes we humans put God to the test, and that was one of them.

When my teacher selected the raffle winner and called out "Walter Johnson," I nearly fell out of my chair. That experience confirmed that little Walter was on God's radar screen. It was exhilarating. Since the day of that grade-school raffle, I've steadfastly sought God's help and blessings when pursuing all my goals. After that, I leave it in God's hands.

While I attended Catholic school from kindergarten through the 12th grade, I remained an Episcopalian along with my mother and father. We attended Calvary Episcopal Church in Charleston, where I was an altar boy.

I remember as a pre-teen when the minister began a series of weekly services in the summer for children. The service was held each Thursday. I rounded up many of the neighborhood kids and marched them to the church for the services. I marshaled them up and maneuvered them through traffic for fourteen city blocks to get them there.

I was in middle school when I first asked my parents if I could switch to Catholicism. The answer was always "no." My senior year I dared to ask my father if I could convert after finishing high school. My mother overheard the conversation and told me later why my father was against me switching to the Catholic faith.

My father at that time was senior warden, treasurer and lay reader at our Episcopal church. He was also a Freemason. Catholics did not join such organizations. So I waited until I was in college and converted to Catholicism.

When I returned home for the Thanksgiving break, I told my father what I had done and he said OK. There was no disappointment as far as I could tell. However, my parents did not go to church that Sunday, which was very unusual. Later that day the Episcopal priest, Father Mackey, came calling to the house.

"Why weren't you in church today?" he asked. "Is there a sickness in the family or any other problems that I should know about?"

Dad told Father Mackey that I had converted to Catholicism while off at college in West Virginia.

"Why did you do it?" the Episcopal priest asked me.

I said I believed Catholicism is the true Church, adding, "Jesus said, 'Upon this rock I will build my church.' He did not say, 'I will build my churches.'"

Father Mackey, my dad and I continued to talk while my mother listened quietly. She rarely spoke freely to anyone other than friends and family because she was sensitive about her lack of a formal education. So I didn't expect her to say a word to Father Mackey, especially because he was an authoritative figure.

But when citing the Bible story about the prodigal son, Father Mackey added, "Some day the black sheep of the Johnson family might come back home."

Mama took great offense.

"You calling my son a black sheep?" she retorted. "My son left home for college and continued to go to church while other kids get away and never see the inside of a sanctuary. And you stand there and say my son is a black sheep?"

Father Mackey left soon thereafter. I looked and Dad and he looked at me and we laughed. But my mother did not think it was funny. My parents participated in all of our children's Catholic baptisms, first Holy Communions and confirmations afterward, and often noted that there was little difference between the faiths.

But one difference that did bother me was the Episcopal Church required everyone to drink from the same chalice during Holy Communion while the Catholic Church made it optional. I never did like drinking from the same cup.

And when I was a child, my mother had a difficult time keeping me in the pew when we attended a church where there was a lot of clapping and loud praying. It's different today. I enjoy black folk Mass in the Catholic Church where there are musicians and the congregation does a lot of clapping and praying aloud. I describe it as a "Batholic Church" celebration — a blend of Baptist and Catholicism. I have come to the conclusion that we are all God's children. People generally worship Him where they are most comfortable. We should pray to overcome our cultural and religious differences and seek a better understanding of one another.

Recently while talking with a classmate at West Virginia State, he said what he remembered most about me was my enthusiasm about going to church. "I would look out the window of my room and you were like a dot running in the snow to catch a ride to church, which was nine miles from campus," he recalled.

Anyway, I've steadfastly sought God's help and blessings when pursuing my goals. After that, I leave it in His hands. The important thing is, after asking God for something, don't insult Him by fretting over it. He heard you the first time!

When I pray, I do so with every fiber of my being. When sending up a prayer, your conviction and faith must come through loud and clear for your own sake. And it doesn't hurt to be specific.

I pray several times a day, not just when I'm facing a crisis. I give thanks mostly, but I'm not afraid to ask for help. I attend church several times a week and I always ask God for strength to handle my failures, setbacks and disappointments. But I'm no "saintly entrepreneur." I'm a sinner like everyone else. I need forgiveness — lots of it.

However, I don't push my religious views on others. Most people I've met are surprised to learn how deeply held my spiritual convictions are. I seldom tote around the Holy Bible and never warn anyone to beware of fire and brimstone. I'm not sure what brimstone is.

My point is, you don't have to be a "Holy Roller" for God to hear you, especially when it comes to business. You don't have to be a cloistered monk either. Do not sit on your you-know-what and try to pray a thriving enterprise into existence. God helps those who are humble and those who get off their rear ends and help themselves.

God, I've had an aggravating day. I allowed events to get the better of me, to set off my temper, and I apologize for that. Thank you for keeping me in good health so that I can tackle my work again tomorrow. Help me perform all of my daily tasks cheerfully and to the best of my ability. Whenever I encounter people, may I be cognizant of your great love for them. And lastly, Lord, by your grace help me overcome my weaknesses and to continue to be appreciative in my faith in you. Amen.

Your prayerful servant,
Wally

Chapter 5

How do you lure top-notch workers to your new business and motivate them to be highly productive while paying them next to nothing? Don't laugh. That's the puzzle practically every new business owner must solve first in order to succeed.

It's a question I faced when I started Eagle Group International in 1995, a year that remains a blur when I look back on it. My energy was directed in a million different directions, dictated by the necessities of bringing in business, nailing down start-up capital and surrounding myself with highly capable people whose services I couldn't afford.

When going after potential staffers, I made it clear that I did not have enough money to pay their salaries. Period. There would be no medical, dental, relocation expenses, tuition reimbursement or company cars. But, I quickly added, when the corporation becomes profitable, I would compensate them well for what they had done. I told them that, if we were as successful as we think we'll be, they would get back pay plus bonuses.

Most of them turned and ran out the door. I would have, too, had I not been so sure of myself by then. Work for someone on the off chance that they might make some money and pay me? Please!

One "perk" I did offer was simple: Members of my team would work out of their homes, not a main office. That's because Eagle Group International didn't have an office at first. Doris and I owned a condo in Atlanta that served the purpose whenever it became necessary for the team to gather in one place. I believed so strongly and passionately in what I was trying to do, I did talk them into it, and with conviction. If you don't buy into your business vision 110 percent, nobody else will.

It took a few weeks to assemble a team of five, including Doris and myself, and I soon began an intense study of the whacky world of government contracts. The three men that I hired were all retired military and they all were white. They were skilled and I knew it because I had served with them in the Army. Remember, when starting a business, surround yourself with people who can do the job regardless of their race or creed or whatever.

All three men were retired Medical Service Corps colonels. Filled with integrity, each was an excellent manager. It bears repeating. If you want to have a successful business, don't get hung up on color or creed. Concentrate on capability and integrity. Many budding entrepreneurs hire only people whose backgrounds and personalities mirror their own. In other words, don't hire your beer-drinking buddies or mall-shopping friends. Each person on your team should have a specific skill that your business needs.

Our first hire worked with a defense contractor at an Army installation in Fort Leavenworth. A native of Georgia, he loved Atlanta and wanted to return. He had a crew cut, no sense of humor and a short temper. He was divorced and said exactly what was on his mind. He was an expert on information technology, manpower issues and contract management. He was also an excellent salesman. When people asked why I put up with his prickly personality, I'd smile and cite his numbers.

The second was also a Georgian whose thick Southern accent was disarming. He was an expert on training issues and an excellent salesman who had earned three master's degrees. He was much smarter than I. If you own a business, do not be intimidated by such employees. It can be good for everyone.

The third worked for me in the Pentagon in a variety of capacities for fifteen years. When he and I were Army colonels, he "watched my back," as they say. He told me who was for me and who was not. Trust and honesty are critical attributes among colleagues in both the military and in private business. This man was the most reluctant to join Eagle Group's original management team. When I contacted him, he said he was retired and had zero desire to work for anyone in any capacity.

"I need somebody I can trust," I said. "I will not take 'no' for an answer." I discovered that I was also a good salesman. He finally agreed to run Eagle Group's day-to-day operations but would not accept pay.

It was a great relief to hire these three men so quickly. But I needed capital to pay lawyers, purchase equipment and office supplies, and cover travel expenses. Getting it would prove to be much harder.

I'm usually optimistic and confident. Yet, when I started Eagle Group International, I harbored a nagging insecurity that was bound to cause trouble. Eventually it did, prompting a business decision that still makes me shudder. Neither my management team nor I had ever run a business before. So I hired an experienced Atlanta health service executive and sold him a significant portion of the company for practically nothing.

We met about a year before I started Eagle Group. Working under the auspices of the American Hospital Association, I had formed the Institute for Diversity in Health Service Management, an Atlanta-based organization whose mission was to help minorities become health-service executives. He and I met for lunch often to discuss business matters. Every time I asked a question about starting a business, his response was quick and accurate.

I began to consider him as a potential business partner. I arranged for Doris to meet him and she liked him too. After some deliberation and a lot of prayer, I asked him if he wanted to be a part owner of Eagle Group International. To my surprise he was interested.

After some preliminary talks, I offered him 25 percent of Eagle Group for $1,000 and he took it. I was ecstatic. The final piece of the puzzle seemed to be in place.

When I formally incorporated Eagle Group International in the state of Georgia, I had a grand total of $4,000 cash, and one-fourth of it came from my new partner. He joined our board of directors. He and I disagreed on a few minor issues, but I deferred to his experience. I reasoned that anything I had to say about business would be theoretical. Surely he knew what he was doing.

During one of our meetings, he and I disagreed on how Eagle Group would be marketed. "Wally, I am the business expert and you are the military expert," he lectured. I stuck to my guns and he reiterated his comment in the same tone of voice. These disagreements continued for weeks and soon became counterproductive.

But I could not sever relations because he owned 25 percent of Eagle Group. So I prayed on it, asking for a resolution that would be to everyone's satisfaction. I never like to settle matters where there is one winner and one loser. I try to create win-win solutions.

With that in mind, I invited our newest partner to lunch so we could talk. "How about putting some more capital into our business?" I asked. "That $4,000 we started out with barely lasted through month No. 1." He hemmed and hawed, clearly not wanting to earmark another penny of his own money for Eagle Group International.

"What's the matter?" I asked. "Don't you think Eagle Group will succeed?"

"I'm not sure," he replied. "The concept is good, but I have my doubts." We talked about his reservations. Ultimately, we got to a point where I asked if I could buy back his share, and he accepted. I borrowed that $1,000 pronto and paid him off. He was happy. I was thrilled. I again owned 100 percent of Eagle Group International.

On one level, though, his departure terrified me. He was the one with all the business experience and he was leaving because he didn't feel Eagle Group would make it. I began having second thoughts about the endeavor.

Two valuable lessons came from this experience. I needed to be more cautious. I decided that I would never share ownership in our company with anyone outside my family. Second, I would divorce emotions from all my business dealings. Just liking someone will get you in trouble. Always be rational in such matters.

Finally, some advice getting investors: More often than not, they'll bring baggage you don't want or need, and they'll probably want to have an undue amount of input regarding your company's operations. Input isn't bad unless it interferes with your vision of where you want your company to go, and what needs to be done to get it there.

My God, thank you for the wisdom I demonstrate in my relations with others. Please continue to help me identify and solve problems as they occur and not let them fester.

Your grateful entrepreneur,
Wally

Chapter 6

My car keys jangled briefly as I pulled into the parking lot and switched off my Chrysler sedan. I checked myself in the rearview mirror and made sure my necktie was straight and there was no lettuce stuck between my teeth. I got out of the car and made sure my pants were zipped up. Show time!

I just knew the first $10,000 in start-up funds I was after would soon be mine. There was no reason to feel anything but confident as I walked toward the Atlanta office of my first potential investor. I was fully prepared to make a formal presentation. Not wanting to weigh Eagle Group down with bank debt, I planned to get private investors to capitalize my new company. Based on my business plan, all I needed was ten at $10,000 apiece and I'd be covered for at least a year and a half.

My prospects were divided into two groups. The first group included former military officers who had high-paying civilian jobs and invested in stocks and real estate. The second was made up of business owners with solid reputations investing in successful ventures. This morning's prospect was a retired Army colonel who worked as a health-service executive. He was waiting at the door when I arrived, which was a very good sign.

"Mild winter we're having," he said with a warm smile and firm handshake. "Please join me in the conference room." I wasted no time setting up my charts and graphs. I gave him a copy of my business plan and ticked off each point of my well-rehearsed presentation. You don't become an Army general officer without having a knack for projecting confidence and authority in such matters. My prospect listened attentively and was obviously impressed.

He asked five questions and I answered each without hesitation. He smiled and nodded and said, "You've got quite an impressive enterprise. Unfortunately, it doesn't dovetail with my investment interests at this time."

Huh?

"Nothing personal, Wally," he said, "but it will take time to build this thing and I don't want to tie up my money for that long."

Although it had been seven years since I left the Army, I still was not used to people telling me "no," regardless of how politely they did it. But when I left that man's office, I wasn't angry. I felt sorry for him. I dangled a fantastic business proposition in front of him and he didn't bite.

I also felt sorry for the next fourteen prospective investors. They didn't bite either. Fifteen prospects, fifteen presentations, fifteen negative responses. I had yet to get a single investment dollar. Each time I was rejected, I prayed for more enthusiasm and energy. It was the first time in my life that I had failed so consistently. I'd always been somewhat successful in my endeavors. When I started delivering newspapers in Charleston as an eighth-grader, I earned a citywide award for gaining the most new subscribers. I'd been an accomplished high school athlete and an excellent student at West Virginia State College, where I earned a degree in zoology.

When I was selected to lead the Medical Service Corps, I advanced over 172 senior officers. The Army Medical Service Corps had more than 5,000 officers worldwide. When promoted to brigadier general, I was appointed director of health services, overseeing the Army Medical Department's planning, medical doctrine, logistics, Reserve and National Guard affairs and field medical support modernization. The modernization budget was over $2 billion. I was the first African American, and the youngest at age 46, to hold both posts, and the first non-physician to direct Army health services operations.

Prayer and hard work had helped me to consistently surmount obstacles and meet lofty expectations all my life. So trying fifteen times and failing fifteen times to get any investors crushed my psyche. I realized something about myself I'd never noticed. I was not a gracious loser. I was irritable and I cursed often. But I never made the mistake of allowing rejection to make me feel unworthy or that God no longer loved me. I've always asked Him to give me the strength to handle setbacks, and, boy, did I need a lot of strength then!

Most of my friends and relatives were of the opinion that leaving a $200,000 job at age 56 was asinine. I heard the whispers. I saw the disapproving looks. I asked Doris if I had let her down.

"Don't worry about it," she said each time I trudged through the door scowling, lugging my charts, graphs and business plans. "You'll hit a home run next time." But by the time I had presented to twenty-six prospective investors, I had whiffed twenty-six times. God and I were having some very serious conversations by then. I asked for strength, but I still felt shaky. I asked for just one victory. I got none. "Why are most entrepreneurs, and especially African-American ones, undercapitalized?" I asked one night as I sat brooding in my study. I felt like an Ethiopian version of Job.

I went to bed but could not sleep. I went to Mass the next morning and asked God to forgive my anger at my weaknesses, and He sent word that we were working on different schedules and that I should have patience. It's amazing how sitting quietly and meditating for an hour in church put things into perspective.

What followed were five more fruitless meetings with potential investors. Thirty-one times I had put on spiffy suits and traveled around the country, smiled broadly and said the right things. And thirty-one times

I walked out empty handed. Getting on intimate terms with failure is a great learning experience. My faith remained strong but my debt was mounting.

Lord, you never, ever said that following you would be easy. I trust you to not give me more pain and frustration that I can bear, and you never have. But if you could please help me understand the circumstances, I sure would appreciate it. Amen.

Your very tired servant,
Wally

Chapter 7

P aranoia is a mental condition. It also results from not having all the facts. On the way to becoming a general in the U.S. Army, a successful health-service executive in the private sector and a multimillionaire, I have encountered numerous liars, cheaters and backstabbers. Fortunately, I have a system of dealing with them. I call it "Positive Paranoia."

I am naturally distrustful. I grew up in poverty in the segregated South. I've known lots of people black and white whose technique for moving forward is to step on everyone who gets in their way. I also know what it's like to be stomped. It's typical of being a person who was born with "a permanent tan."

When I was an Army captain, I served a stint as a teacher at the Medical Field Service School in Fort Sam Houston, Texas. I was the only African American on the teaching staff. Virtually all the students were white physicians, dentists and others who were highly educated in medicine and other health-related fields. They were regular Army and Reservists on active duty at that time. Each was smart and knew it. They reminded me of the character Hawkeye Pierce, the cocky physician in the MASH movie and television series. A respect for military authority was not a priority for most of them.

So there I stood at the podium inside Fort Sam Houston's Medical Field Services School classroom feeling confident about my knowledge of the subject matter yet knowing I would be tested once the class began. I was supposed to teach these people something but some wanted to teach me.

The reputation of an entire race rested squarely on my shoulders along with my captain's bars. It was like being a speck of bacteria under a giant electron microscope. So I carefully prepared for each class, and those smart young students challenged me. Some of them asked me questions designed to trick or embarrass me. When I jokingly mentioned this to my supervising officer, he said, with a smile, that I had a case of paranoia.

One day my supervisor decided to monitor my class. He sat in the back of the classroom for about forty minutes and left. After class, I went by his office, as was the custom when the boss monitored the class. I was expecting a critique of my content and demeanor. He arose from his seat, came from around his desk and with a hearty laugh, looked straight into my eyes and said, "You are right. They do ask you the darnedest questions."

But I answered those students' questions, usually in a humorous manner. I had prepared myself for that job and everyone in the room knew it. That's what paranoia does for someone like me. It forces me to be ready and on guard. Whenever I'm in charge of a group, I assess each of the members individually the best I can to determine which ones will attempt to make me look bad or may not be totally committed to my team and me. Always ask yourself, "Should I trust this person?" Then do your job.

When I was growing up in Charleston, my father decided that I needed more education and a change of scenery. So he insisted that I spend my summers with aunts and uncles who lived in Harlem, N.Y., and in Patterson, N.J.

"Son, in addition to being book smart you also need to be street smart to succeed in this world," he told me.

The streets of Harlem are great classrooms. As soon as the kids there found out I was from the South, the games began. They would try to "get over" on me daily with one challenge after another. I quickly learned to see those schemes coming, avoid embarrassment and pretend that nothing happened. "Street smart" is being able to quickly read people and understand from where they are coming. It's the ability to assess people — especially their body language — and anticipate their next move. Essentially, it's developing extraordinary common sense.

It was also during this time in New York City that my uncle, a merchant seaman who rarely worked, took me to see baseball great Joe DiMaggio play in Yankee Stadium. We also visited Ellis Island. I climbed to the top of the Statue of Liberty. He taught me how to gamble and when he won enough money from me to buy a can of beer, he sent me to the store to purchase it.

My uncle in New Jersey was just the opposite. He had the same work ethic as my father. He drove a road grader for a construction company and worked in a bakery at night. He owned a dump truck and delivered dirt on weekends. He could not say "no" to friends and relatives. I was 16 years old when he gave me my first automobile, a 1949 Ford convertible. Soon afterward, he was helping a neighbor cut down a tree and fell to his death. He was a remarkable man.

Both my aunt in New Jersey and my aunt in Harlem were excellent seamstresses. As I said, most members of my family were exceptionally hard-working people who meant a lot to me when I was growing up.

I was a successful athlete in my youth. Every day in the projects I played basketball, baseball and football with kids my age and older. When it came time to choose up sides, I was always selected to play on a team. I gained a lot of confidence by being a good athlete. This is important, especially among African Americans. For many disadvantaged kids, excelling in sports is one of a few ways to obtain an education and escape poverty.

I learned as a young African-American second lieutenant assigned to the elite 82nd Airborne Division that being recognized for performance as I competed with my colleagues, most of them white, was not easy. Time and time again, I had to excel in order to be accepted as an equal. Once I got used to going above and beyond the norm, I asked myself, "Why stop?"

The man who helped me elevate my technique of "positive paranoia" to an art form was Gen. Maxwell Thurman, the Army's vice chief of staff and a four-star commander. He was the brightest, most intelligent and most dedicated officer I have ever met. He knew the Headquarters Department of the Army inside out. He created and established many of the systems now used to structure, equip, fund, staff, maintain and modernize the war-fighting capabilities of the best military organization in the world.

I briefed Gen. Thurman on numerous occasions. He knew the right questions to ask. If the person briefing him lied, he caught him. If someone he asked a question guessed at an answer, he corrected him. Many officers on the staff went to extraordinary lengths to avoid having to brief Gen. Thurman. You had to know the subject when you briefed him. You would be fired or embarrassed or both if you did not.

I was a young major when I met the man in 1972. Every time I briefed him, I was ready. Even today, when preparing for a job, I ask, "OK, Wally. Would you make this presentation to Gen. Thurman?" If the answer is "no," I'll rework it. If "yes," I present it with confidence.

Oh my God, thank you for helping me use my positive paranoia as an effective management tool and to my advantage.
Your cautious servant,
Wally

Chapter 8

I f you've worked a nine-to-five job most of your life, you are not prepared for the rollercoaster ride of entrepreneurship. Like most first-time business owners, I didn't know what I was getting into. There were times when I simply cradled my head in my hands and pleaded, "Help me, Jesus!"

Most new entrepreneurs receive the sternest tests of their resolve and management abilities during their first twelve months of operation. All new business owners want everything to run smoothly, which is unrealistic. As painful as pitfalls and obstacles are to deal with, though, they engage managerial muscles never before flexed, especially those needed to improve problem-solving abilities.

Case in point: I had a significant problem convincing investors to join Eagle Group. But there are many ways to clear an obstacle even though it may not be obvious. Sometimes, the best way to arrive at a solution is to step back a bit and study the situation, which I found out by accident. Or maybe divine intervention is more accurate.

Frustrated because of insufficient operating capital, I figured it was time for a "fishing only" weekend. So Doris and I drove from Atlanta to Georgetown one beautiful Saturday morning and set out on our 37-foot cabin cruiser, which we kept docked in the canal behind our house. Our "fishing only" getaway had one rule: Talking business was off-limits.

Chilling on the deck of our boat, being nearly lulled to sleep by the sound of water lapping against its hull, relaxed my mind. Like a lot of new business owners, I had attached a life-or-death importance to Eagle Group. Piloting our boat helped me depressurize and put things back into perspective.

That's when it hit me.

"I think we need to sell the boat," I blurted out.

We hadn't been on the water three hours and here I was breaking my self-imposed moratorium on Eagle Group conversation. But I had just had an epiphany – I could sell the yacht and get some operating capital.

I certainly loved my boat and got tremendous pleasure from it, but neither Doris nor I have ever been wedded to material things. Plus, I was confident that I would one day be able to buy another — bigger — yacht once I got business on track

Doris not only agreed but also suggested we take out second mortgages on our condo in Atlanta and our house in South Carolina. Now that's confidence! Anyway, our children had always kidded us that they'd be paying off our bills long after our demise, so I had my excuse lined up.

I called a local boat broker that afternoon to find a buyer who was willing to make a low-ball offer. Surprisingly, it didn't take long to find one. I wasn't pleased with his $60,000 offer — but I didn't have time to haggle — so I sold it.

When I visited my local banker, Danny Siau, I asked him about securing a second mortgage on my Georgetown home. I had with me a notebook of more than six pages of potential customers. I explained to Danny the type of work associated with each potential customer.

When I was finished, Danny asked if I knew anything about real estate. I answered in the affirmative. He looked me squarely in the eyes and said, "Those potential customers you have in that notebook are like real estate listings and the bank doesn't make loans based on listings. He then said, "Let's see what you have in that house on the canal." After an appraisal and other paperwork, I had another $100,000 in operating cash. The second mortgage was actually a third, as we had a previous second mortgage on the house.

After receiving the third mortgage on our home, Doris quipped that we will wake up one morning and Danny and his family will be living in our house.

While I may have been successful in the past in a variety of jobs, no one was willing to invest any money up front on this venture. My wife and I were the only ones willing to take the financial risk and we placed practically everything on the line, including my 401K savings. But we had faith in my ability to succeed despite the odds.

My failure to nail down a single investor was actually a blessing. I learned a lesson. When you experience a setback, 98 times out of 100, there is a silver lining. Just relax, clear your mind, ask God for help and listen. He will answer. Taking stock in the old saying, "Necessity is the mother of invention," along with innovative and creative financing, will keep you in business.

Ernest and loving God,

Thanks for an understanding wife who agreed to put most of our material possessions on the line and for a partner who believed that with your help our entrepreneurial venture will succeed in one way or another.

Your appreciative entrepreneur,

Wally

Doris Wright and
Wally Johnson
in 1957 on the
night of the high
school prom.

Wally today and at age 5 in front of
his home in Gadsen Green projects
in Charleston, S.C.

Second Lieutenant Wally Johnson in combat gear and parachutes at Pope Air Force Base, Fayetteville, N.C.

First Lieutenant Johnson in 1963.

Brigadier General Glenn Collins, commander of the 44th Medical Brigade, presents Captain Wally Johnson a plaque during his Bronze Star Medal ceremony.

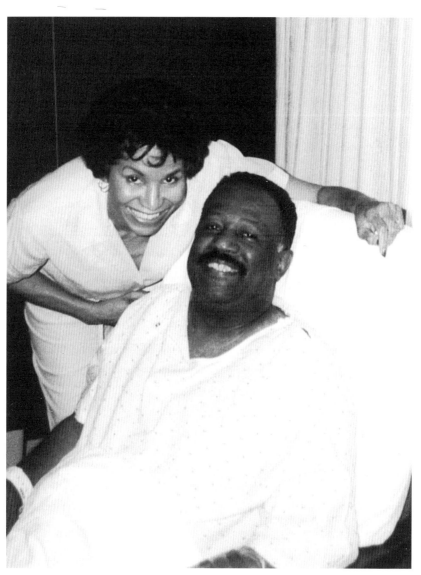

Doris and Wally, a day after surgery at Walter Reed Army Medical Center.

Brigadier General Wally Johnson.

Wally, Doris, Wally's father Walter F. Johnson Jr. and his mother Inez Johnson.

Below, from left to right, Wally and Doris with their children A.J., Roxy, Wally IV, Rhoda and T. Fitz. At right, an inset of Ian, who was in neurosurgery residency at Harvard University, Brigham and Women's Medical Center.

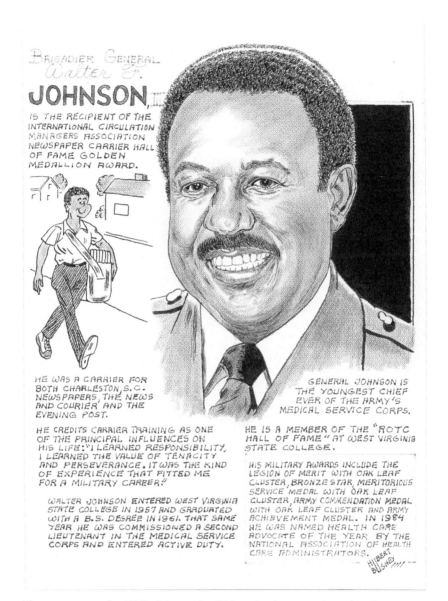

BRIGADIER GENERAL Walter F.

JOHNSON, III

IS THE RECIPIENT OF THE INTERNATIONAL CIRCULATION MANAGERS ASSOCIATION NEWSPAPER CARRIER HALL OF FAME GOLDEN MEDALLION AWARD.

HE WAS A CARRIER FOR BOTH CHARLESTON, S.C. NEWSPAPERS, THE NEWS AND COURIER AND THE EVENING POST.

HE CREDITS CARRIER TRAINING AS ONE OF THE PRINCIPAL INFLUENCES ON HIS LIFE: "I LEARNED RESPONSIBILITY, I LEARNED THE VALUE OF TENACITY AND PERSEVERANCE. IT WAS THE KIND OF EXPERIENCE THAT FITTED ME FOR A MILITARY CAREER."

WALTER JOHNSON ENTERED WEST VIRGINIA STATE COLLEGE IN 1957 AND GRADUATED WITH A B.S. DEGREE IN 1961. THAT SAME YEAR HE WAS COMMISSIONED A SECOND LIEUTENANT IN THE MEDICAL SERVICE CORPS AND ENTERED ACTIVE DUTY.

GENERAL JOHNSON IS THE YOUNGEST CHIEF EVER OF THE ARMY'S MEDICAL SERVICE CORPS.

HE IS A MEMBER OF THE "ROTC HALL OF FAME" AT WEST VIRGINIA STATE COLLEGE.

HIS MILITARY AWARDS INCLUDE THE LEGION OF MERIT WITH OAK LEAF CLUSTER, BRONZE STAR, MERITORIOUS SERVICE MEDAL WITH OAK LEAF CLUSTER, ARMY COMMENDATION MEDAL WITH OAK LEAF CLUSTER AND ARMY ACHIEVEMENT MEDAL. IN 1984 HE WAS NAMED HEALTH CARE ADVOCATE OF THE YEAR BY THE NATIONAL ASSOCIATION OF HEALTH CARE ADMINISTRATORS.

HILBERT BUSHEY

Plaque presented to Wally Johnson in 1988 noting he was selected to the International Newspaper Carrier Hall of Fame.

Chapter 9

When starting your own business, be sure to develop a comprehensive business plan. Once I did that, I knew that Eagle Group International was severely undercapitalized.

A well-thought-out business plan forces you to be creative. The safe, low-risk approach that I took initially was no longer relevant. Being an entrepreneur is about survival of the fittest, and in business, the fittest out-think and out-execute their competitors. And when all of your own hard-earned money is on the line, it's wise to become "fiscally fit," if you know what I mean.

I have used what I call "the question technique" effectively through the years as part of my planning process. Today, it's second nature for me. It keeps me out of trouble, especially when starting a new project. These questions are not a substitute for thorough planning, just an initial step to get the process going.

I usually ask myself, "What do we believe in and what do we stand for?" This is how I develop the VISION for the endeavor.

Then, I ask, "What are members of my team going to do as a group?" This determines the MISSION.

"What do we see as our future?" This determines our GOALS.

"How are we going to get there?" With STRATEGIES.

"What do we need to succeed?" This helps us determine our RESOURCES.

And finally, "What are our STRENGTHS, WEAKNESSES,

OPPORTUNITIES and THREATS?" The acronym for these questions is SWOT, which is commonly used in business plans.

When these questions are answered, I have enough information to write first an action plan, which is followed by a business plan. This approach, if done thoroughly, covers all the bases, so to speak. Once you compile this information and get it in order, it's important to get your managers and employees involved. By giving them responsibility, you are giving each a sense of empowerment. They have a stake in the process and the basis for making more and more independent decisions that are necessary for success.

But it's very important that each employee is not wasteful with your investment.

Jesus had no problem with being frugal. Neither did Doris and I. We seldom went out to eat unless we had to. Taking a vacation was out of the question. We made do with what we had.

We sold our condominium in Atlanta and rented a reasonably priced hotel room instead. We slept there and it served as our home office. Needless to say, I spent a lot of time on the roads between Georgetown, Atlanta and Washington, D.C. where most of my business contacts were. Flying would have saved time. But time I had. Money, I did not.

Doris and I actually enjoyed our new nomadic lifestyle. "Fine cuisine" was the difference between Mickey D's and the Cracker Barrel. Whenever we traveled to Washington, D.C., we chose economy lodging. We were like newlyweds again.

Of course it was stressful at times. For us, being broke was like taking a long camping trip, never sure where we would pitch the tent, always wondering if a grizzly bear might stop by for supper.

When starting a new business, make sure your spouse is in for the long haul. I thank God every day that Doris continues to share the same tent with me. Like the Bible says, marriage is when two people join each other and become a whole new being, each having his and her own personality, but living and working as one.

Sometimes when we traveled to Washington in search of contracts, even staying at a Days Inn was out of the question because of our budget. So we stayed with Uncle Gilbert and Aunt Brenda in their suburban Virginia townhouse. This was a good thing in more ways than one. We were careful not to wear out our welcome and we had fun! We also knew that, if we stayed in fancy hotels, we shouldn't demand that other members of Eagle Group's executive group sleep cheap while on the road.

Fact is, Doris and I were rich. We had our health and our children and happiness. We knew we could count on God, our loving uncles and aunts other relatives, and our friends.

Almighty and merciful God, who has commissioned angels to guide and protect us, may they be our companions from our setting out until our return. Clothe us with their invisible protection; keep from us all danger of collision, of fire, of explosion, of falling; and finally, having preserved us from evil, and especially from sin, guide us to our heavenly home.

Your traveling entrepreneur,

Wally

Chapter 10

Before I launched Eagle Group, an entrepreneur friend warned it is much easier to start a business in your 20s than in your 50s. I dismissed her advice. Now I know better.

Throughout 1996 into 1997, "Mr. Big Time Entrepreneur" — that's me — was worn out. But had I complained to Doris, she would have said: "Whose fault is that? You must take care of yourself. Make a doctor's appointment by the end of the month."

I was working harder than I did before I left the military in 1988. I was in what seemed to be a never-ending race against time. I had to dig deep for the willpower to stay in the running. My weight plummeted and my hair thinned. It's difficult to generate the same energy and stamina at age 56 that seemed so effortless at 36.

When I pray for strength, I more often than not ask for physical staying power. By the way, if you think being ridiculously busy is an excuse not to pray, you couldn't be more wrong. It's just the opposite.

And I did not ask God to help me grow Eagle Group to a specific dollar value. My initial objective was $1 million in revenue after the first year of operation, but that was arbitrary. My intent was to grow Eagle Group to the maximum the market would allow.

A successful entrepreneur I knew said I was arrogant. I disagreed. I was determined. I was climbing Mount Everest, not some hill of beans. Why in the world would I take all of this aggravation for a slim salary increase?

I first encountered this troubling mindset at a meeting at the Charleston (S.C.) Air Force Base. It was in a conference room filled with minority contractors wanting to land government business. Lots of white women were there. Under the federal government guidelines, women are considered a minority too.

I was struck by the way the person from the contracting office who led the discussion focused exclusively on obtaining contracts valued at $1,000 or lower. I thought she was joking. She was not. Are they subliminally limiting minority contractors to a dollar amount, I wondered. I decided to find out.

I wanted to learn how to secure contracts worth tens of thousands of dollars. When the meeting ended, everyone seemed to accept the session leader's low expectations. They asked no questions and left. I was stunned. I'd just as soon get another 9-to-5 for such a pittance.

The room was empty when I approached the seminar leader and asked her how to attract contract work worth more than $1,000. She said she could not help me. If I wanted anything larger than $1,000, then I should go to her office and read the bulletin board, she said condescendingly. Her response was as disappointing as her demeanor. I was a gentleman but I was not happy. I did not drive from Atlanta to Charleston to be brushed off, especially by a low-level bureaucrat.

Remember, if you are turned away as I was, make sure it's by someone in authority. Never accept "no" from anyone who can't give you the green light in the first place. I asked her one more time if she could help me obtain work that brought in more than $1,000, and again she declined.

So I went to see her supervisor, an Air Force officer. When I explained to him what had happened, he apologized but was no more helpful. I left with no useful information about how to secure significant federal contracts. But I did let him know that they needed to get their act together concerning minority contractors. He said he would.

I fumed as I began my 320-mile trip back to Atlanta. Then I prayed.

This is what I normally do anyway if I'm in the car for 15 minutes or 10 hours. I pray the rosary, a repetitive prayer to Jesus' mother, for clarity and I pray for strength and I pray for guidance. And, of course, I do so with my eyes wide open.

God, I'm keeping both my hands on the wheel and driving defensively as I pray to you. With you there is no such thing as wasted time or a wasted trip. I know you've put me in this situation to teach me something. But I'm feeling dense today, so please grant me the wisdom to understand what was going on back there.

Your safe-driving servant,
Wally

Chapter 11

W hat I'm about to say next will upset some folks, but it's true. White businessmen have benefited from "affirmative action" from day one of our great republic. They just don't call it "affirmative action."

This is understandable. If African Americans or Hispanic Americans or whatever Americans held the power, they too would give preferential treatment to those they understand the best. That's clearly the case with the Cuban Americans in Miami today.

So why shouldn't a gentleman of African descent who grew up in Charleston, S.C., where an estimated 40 percent of all America's original slaves arrived to be sold on the auction block, take advantage of affirmative action too? Succeeding in business is about capitalizing on every competitive advantage at one's disposal, right?

It certainly is. I sent a company director, a white man, to apply for Eagle Group International's minority-owned business certificate from the City of Atlanta. He got some odd looks. But, fact is, he worked for me and I was a black owner ready to do business.

Of course, the bureaucrat who took the application assumed it was a scam, and, sure enough, several city officials demanded to meet with me personally before certifying Eagle Group International as a minority business. I accepted the skepticism. Indeed, there have been instances in Atlanta and elsewhere where white business owners try to take advantage of minority set-asides in such a way.

So Doris, the white company director and I met with the bureaucrats to set the record straight. After proving beyond a doubt that I am who I am, I asked if they thought my request was bogus, and they said they did, initially, because my representative had given his home address and phone number when he first arrived at the city office, then listed my address and phone number on the application.

The three of us began laughing, and the more the stone-faced bureaucrats glared at us, the more we laughed. It wasn't good public relations, but we could not help it.

We got that certificate. And it was not the only time we had trouble getting minority certifications. But we got them because we were honest.

My next step was to become a federally certified minority business under the Small Business Administration's 8(a) Business Development program. It was created to help small businesses access the federal procurement arena. The paperwork is excessive. Even old Job of Bible fame would have cussed about it.

I articulated a few choice phrases as I tackled one agonizingly detailed 8(a) document after another. How was I supposed to know exactly who my ancestors were, from where they came, when they arrived in this country and how they got here? But I rolled up my sleeves and plowed steadily through bureaucratic muck like my ancestors surely did in the mud after they landed in America.

I could not count the number of times potential customers said they couldn't give Eagle Group a federal contract because we weren't 8(a) certified. But we finally succeeded after many months of work.

In case you've ever wondered if God has a sense of humor, remember the fuss I made over the advisor at Charleston Air Force Base who encouraged minorities to go after contracts less than $1,000? Well, the very first contract Eagle Group International secured through its 8(a) connection was for $400.

But perseverance paid off. Not long afterward, 8(a) contracts for tens of thousands of dollars came in, and I wasn't surprised. Faith, determination and hard work are critical. However, there is a misconception that 8(a) contracts are set-asides. To the contrary, most contracts are awarded through competitive bids.

As we generated more and more income, our arbitrary $1 million revenue goal rose to $3 million annually. It was divine. Seriously. Angels came to me at that time. One is Martha Alford, my executive assistant. She kept the glory train running on time, and I thank God for her. Contracts ranging from $20,000 to $70,000 rolled in and our staff grew from five employees to 46.

We were making enough to pay them and to keep the lights on, and our revenues were increasing steadily. We were planting seeds and cultivating clients and a big harvest was sure to come. With each contract, we under-bid and provided superior service. We always gave the customer more than what was required in the contract.

Government bureaucrats don't take risks. They don't sign off on large contracts to new companies for fear the deals will fail and they will lose their jobs. So, I gladly accepted small contracts and made sure that Eagle Group's performance was exemplary. This put the bureaucrats at ease and cleared the way for bigger contracts.

Remember, your reputation is important. Be honest. Be thorough. And beware — especially when hiring because it is an inexact science.

Honesty and integrity are the keys to our success. Our clients trusted us. "Thou Shall Not Bear False Witness" is one of the Ten Commandments, and for good reason, especially when running a business. Do not tell lies and do not keep employees who tell lies. That's what making "an honest buck" is all about. The first employee we released was because she lied.

Also make sure everyone who works with you understands frugality.

I have no sympathy for those who do not appreciate the importance of being wise when spending my money.

I once served as host for an important, civilian, non-government client. Three members of my team accompanied me to a fancy Atlanta restaurant for this occasion. Two of my folks and I ordered chicken, the cheapest item on the menu. The fourth got filet mignon. Eagle Group had not risen to "prime beef" status yet, and that person knew it.

A couple of weeks later, several of us visited a customer at Fort Knox, Ky. It was not long after we got to town that "Mr. Filet Mignon" advised us that we needed to stop by Kinko's to make copies of some important documents we planned to leave with our clients.

It takes a lot to make me angry, and this man had done it.

"Why didn't you make copies on our machine back at the office?" I asked.

"Didn't think about it until now," he said. "No big deal."

Needless to say, "Mr. Chopped Liver" was soon out of a job.

You will not succeed as an entrepreneur if you or your employees have a selfish sense of entitlement. Spend your company's money wisely, and make sure your employees do the same. I did when I worked for both the government and the American Hospital Association. And it paid off.

I praise you Father for helping me to wisely use all the resources you provide me and I thank you for instilling in me a solid and good value system.
Frugally yours,
Wally

Chapter 12

Few people know this about me. I have bad credit. Show me an entrepreneur with a 700 credit score, and I'll show you someone who probably has inherited wealth.

Even though I've never defaulted on a loan, my score has been terrible since I was in the Army. My credit numbers tumbled steadily while we scrambled to get four of our children through college simultaneously on my military salary.

I also had a tax problem resulting from a real estate transaction. State tax officials said we owed money. I disagreed. After four months of this, the tax-office geniuses — I use the descriptive sarcastically — caused me to get four months behind in my mortgage payments. My credit score was radioactive by then. Nobody would loan me anything, it seemed.

After I started Eagle Group, my credit worthiness spiraled downward even more. I was paying my mortgage every other month as I struggled to get my company up and running. But having bad credit scores is not a valid excuse for not starting your own business.

By all means, keep your scores up. But if they are low, it's not impossible to borrow money. I decided to get to know my banker personally because lending money is based primarily on trust, not some three-digit number a credit bureau assigns you. So, if you have a bad credit score, unleash your creative juices and let them flow. Go see your banker and convince him that you are not a bad risk.

A banker I once knew told me that 80 percent of determining whether to lend money has to do with trust and the rest with regulations. Once a loan officer determines that you are a good risk, he or she can get around the regulations.

But once you get a loan, do not fail to pay it off in full, which includes interest. REPEAT: ALWAYS PAY YOUR LOAN OFF IN FULL, IN-CLUDING INTEREST. Being late is one thing. Not paying it off is another. I've never taken out a loan that I failed to repay in full. My word is my bond when it comes to borrowing money. And my advice to loan officers is, "Better late than never."

My Beloved Father,

Thanks very much for giving me strength to persevere. You are my light as I navigate through the darkness of life.

Your sometimes-slow-but-sure servant,

Wally

Chapter 13

The concept of "family" is the foundation upon which Eagle Group International was constructed.

Too often African-American entrepreneurs create viable companies without grooming anyone to succeed them. If the company founder then dies or is incapacitated in some way, the enterprise quickly unravels.

Eagle Group was established to satisfy two family-oriented objectives. I wanted it to be controlled by relatives after I stepped down and I wanted to create wealth that the next generations of my family could use to be happy and to prosper.

Nepotism, in my opinion, is a good thing when practiced properly. I am very aware that this opinion goes against the grain of what people consider good business. But a close family member is less likely to cheat you. Also, kinfolk usually join the company knowing a good deal about your business. And relatives are more likely to hold themselves to a higher performance standard. That's what I've learned about my family, as well as the members of the Eagle Group family of families.

But use some common sense in this regard. You don't want to make cousin Pookie, the con artist, corporate treasurer!

Of course, nepotism will torpedo employee morale if it is not practiced properly. Do not show favoritism to family members who do not have the skills to move your company forward.

I believe strongly in family, and that goes beyond biological relationships. I did everything possible for my staff to feel and believe they belonged to the Eagle Group family. Whenever I gave a talk about the company, I make it a point to mention the Eagle Group family. I encouraged my key executives to consider hiring their own relatives to fill vacant positions.

My son A.J. — a graduate of Texas Tech University who also has a doctorate degree in law and a master's degree in business administration from George Washington University — joined Eagle Group in 1998 and soon became vice president for finance. In 2004 he became president.

Not long afterward, son Terrell — a graduate of The Citadel in Charleston, with a master's degree in education from Troy State University and a law degree from the University of Kentucky — told me he wanted to join the company after graduating from law school. I insisted that Terrell first work for a year in a law firm, which he did.

Terrell also was a U.S. Army officer and had more than ten years of military service in the area of medical operations and human resources. He retired from the Reserves as a major and joined Eagle Group as vice president for human resources and legal counsel. He became Eagle Group's CEO in 2004. I should also note that Terrell got his undergraduate degree from that formerly all-white and all-male S.C. military college just down the street from the public housing projects where I lived as a child.

Today, right in the middle of the Gadsden Green housing complex — Charleston's largest public housing community — is a bright ray of sunshine. The Charleston Development Academy Public Charter School, directed by Cecilia Gordon Rogers, is in its sixth year of helping children who live in the area. The school offers kindergarten through seventh grade classes and its students have won numerous statewide academic awards, especially in mathematics. Times have changed, thank God.

Currently, A.J. handles the family's investments as president and CEO of Georgetown Capital Management.

Other Eagle Group executives include my oldest son, Walter IV, who attended Northern Virginia College, and my daughters RoxAnne and Rhoda, both graduates of the University of South Carolina.

Walter IV, president of Eagle Automotive, operated four family-owned automotive tire and repair stores in the greater Atlanta area.

Roxy, an Eagle Group executive, worked as president of Johnson Management Company with land acquisition and other real estate projects.

Rhoda, who also has a master's degree in education from Central Michigan State University, taught school in Charleston before joining Eagle Group. She was co-director of a Job Corps contract administered through the U.S. Department of Labor.

Our only child operating outside the Eagle Group orbit is Ian, a Harvard-trained neurosurgeon who graduated from the University of Virginia and the University of Louisville Medical School.

Ian's wife, Angela, who graduated from the University of Virginia and has a master's degree in health services administration from the University of Kentucky and a law degree from the University of Louisville, was our company's legal counsel.

Rhoda's husband, Alfred, a University of South Carolina graduate in electrical engineering, became an Eagle Group vice president for information technology.

Our two daughters and four daughters-in-law currently are board members of the Walter and Doris Johnson Charitable Foundation. My wife, Doris, who is a graduate of Spelman College, is the chairperson of the foundation.

Our other daughters-in-law are Debra, who graduated from the University of Kentucky with undergraduate and graduate degrees in social work; Judy, who graduated from St. Mary's College with a degree in English literature; and Debora, who graduated from the Connecticut School of Broadcasting.

Lord, you know I believe charity begins at home and I thank you for such wonderful children. I am grateful that you have provided me with a strong belief and a need for a solid educational foundation in addition to the exquisite jewels you have provided me in the form of my children.

Your family man,
Wally

Chapter 14

I underwent my annual physical in March 1998, three years to the month after I started Eagle Group. Being around doctors when I worked in the Army Medical Department impressed upon me the importance of getting an annual checkup.

Like most men over 50, there is one procedure I dread more than any other. Nothing is pleasant about having your prostate gland examined. So there I was in the doctor's office, naked from the waist down, reassuring myself that what was good about this procedure is that it would be another year before I had to go though the humiliation again.

"Seems normal," my family doctor said once the deed was done and he removed the rubber glove. "We'll give you a call when we get the lab results."

He was referring to the number that specified my prostate specific antigen, or PSA, which is determined with a routine blood test for older men. Three days later while at work in Atlanta, I checked my messages. My family doctor's assistant had left one asking me to call her. Her tone was pleasant but direct. I knew something was wrong. I thought about my father, who at age 77 died of complications caused by prostate cancer.

My father was still young when he passed a Civil Service exam and became a postal worker. He worked hard through the years, opened a music shop with two colleagues, started a snack-food vending company, was a Boy Scout troop master, was the church treasurer, helped organize Charleston's Colored Men Business Association and served as its first president.

He later became an agent with the North Carolina Mutual Insurance Company in Charleston, which specialized in coverage for African Americans. He worked as a manager for the company in Columbia, S.C., Chattanooga, Tenn., and Philadelphia, Pa. But after working for eight years as manager of the Philadelphia district, he suffered a stroke. He recovered from that but retired soon afterward and returned to Charleston.

He soon landed another job as a court bailiff in his hometown. Seven years to the day after he suffered his stroke, my father was working in the courtroom and experienced severe chest pains. He left the courthouse, flagged down a cab and asked to be taken to the hospital emergency room. He told the emergency room nurse that he thought he had had a heart attack. After the doctor's examination and the lab results confirmed that he had indeed suffered a heart attack.

I soon arrived and asked my father why he didn't call for an ambulance. "Too expensive," he said.

He recovered from that and returned to work. It was in 1994 that he was diagnosed with end-stage prostate cancer and he died shortly afterward. My father was a good man. He especially loved to act and played roles in several plays. But his most successful role was that of a loving father and husband. And he starred at that until the day he died.

Anyway, I returned the call to my doctor's assistant, who answered the phone. I told her who I was and she put me on hold as the music of singer Barry Manilow droned on and on in the background. I was not a big Barry Manilow fan. I am even less so now. The doctor finally picked up and I listened carefully:

"Wally. Your PSA has risen. Given the fact that your father had prostate cancer, you need to see a urologist."

I did as I was instructed. The urologist did an ultrasound and noted, "You have a little spot there," as we viewed the monitor. "The chance of that being cancerous is about 20 percent, maybe 25. I'll have to do a biopsy."

I did not obsess over this terrible news. I was too busy. Too many things were happening with Eagle Group International at that time. I was at my desk at work three days later when the phone rang.

It was the doctor. He said the biopsy was positive. I had prostate cancer in an early stage of development, he explained. I remembered clearly the urologist saying not to go crazy, "We can handle this."

"Are you sure?"

"Yes, I'm sorry. No question about it."

"OK," I responded. "Thanks."

The first thing I thought about as I hung up the phone was why I thanked that man. He had just given me the worst news possible and I thanked him for it! Then I thought about my dear parents, who insisted that I express my appreciation when someone does something for me. It just came automatic.

However, the diagnosis did not come as a great surprise. When I was in the Army Medical Department, I was chief of staff for the Surgeon General, an urologist, who often said, "Wally, if you live long enough, you'll probably have prostate cancer. You won't necessarily die from it, but you'll get it."

Older men are hearing this nowadays. I just didn't think it would get me at age 59. So I sat there at my desk in my office in Atlanta and wondered about what I should do next. I did not contact my wife at that time but I did call on God. I prayed the rosary during my routine walk, then asked for personal advice from God. And he heard me.

We decided that I should wait until I got home so I could tell Doris face-to-face. For the rest of that day at the office, I did what I needed to do. No one had a clue, I thought, as I headed out the front door, climbed into my car, strapped myself in and drove home.

I thought about how my father fought courageously until he could fight no more. I recalled watching handsome, robust Walter F. Johnson Jr. waste away. I thought about how my family physician joked that he was duty-bound to keep me alive until at least age 77 like my dad.

I did not want to die so soon. So I asked God to work with me on this one, and we agreed that I should do everything that I could to get myself physically fit and try to keep my body from betraying me. My children still needed me, and I had a loving wife with whom I could grow old. I had future grandchildren to meet.

Serious health challenges force entrepreneurs to put everything into perspective. A company may seem like the be all and end all when you're well, but it quickly gets pushed to the background when your life is on the line. Facing death crystallizes what is and what is not of paramount importance.

Doris was waiting for me as I opened the front door. She had a premonition that something was wrong. She handled the news like she does most things — with an extraordinary sense of calmness. But fear was in her eyes. She could not hide it.

We soon discussed specifics of my problem, the treatment options, the pluses and minuses, and we re-confirmed our marriage vows.

"Walter, medical science has come a long way since your dad died," she said, holding one of my hands between hers. "We can beat this thing. We will get through this."

God, I love this woman!

I asked Doris not to say anything to the children about it. We agreed that we did not want them to worry. Worry is a wasted emotion. Besides, I didn't want my children interrogating me. I already had too much to think about.

The children were not the only ones who did not know at that time. All but my top two executives at Eagle Group International would be kept in the dark about my condition. In the military, top-secret information is shared on a strict need-to-know basis. The fight for my life would be handled in the same way.

When we arrived back in Georgetown, she accompanied me to the urologist's office and queried him intensely. He said my prostate could be removed surgically in a procedure called a "prostatectomy." Or I could undergo radiation treatments, including a new technique in which radioactive seeds would be planted inside my scrotum to directly assault the cancer cells.

He also said an operation could render me impotent permanently.

"I want it cut out," I said. "I want to get the cancer now!"

"You want me to schedule an operating room?" he asked.

I looked at Doris and she looked at me, and I said, "OK." He scheduled the operation for May.

I won't say that he was not as concerned as I was, but he didn't see any need to speed it up. I wanted the surgery the next day. So, since I had an ongoing friendship with a very talented urologist in Texas, why shouldn't I call him and ask what he thought?

Fact is, I had access to urologists who cared for the President of the United States and members of Congress. I'd be crazy not to take advantage of my service to my country as the head of the U.S. Army Medical Service Corps.

Doris and I were silent during the drive back home. As soon as I opened the front door of our house, I headed to my study and called Bernie Mittemeyer, a former Army Surgeon General who was chancellor of Texas Tech University Medical School at that time. I wasted no time getting to the point.

"Wally, you need to go to Walter Reed Army Hospital in Washington, D.C.," he said. "Col. Ronald McLeod works there. He's the best in the world. He has cared for presidents of the United States, members of Congress and many others."

Until then, I had not pulled rank to take advantage of my military service. But this was different. I would take full advantage now. I earned it. My life was on the line.

Col. McLeod agreed to do the prostatectomy and scheduled me for July 1998, four months after I had been diagnosed with cancer. I would be staying in a hospital suite reserved for two-star generals and higher because Walter F. Johnson III was a retired Army Medical Department general officer, thank God.

I had no problem with this. I gave Uncle Sam 110 percent every minute I served in the Army, and I deserved the best medical care available.

In the weeks leading up to my surgery, I made sure that Doris knew how I felt about her. She is an incredible blessing in my life. She has never let me down. I also made sure that Eagle Group International could continue to function properly without me for a while.

However, I erred when I did not make it clear who would succeed me if I did not survive. It's great to think positive, but when running a business, you must prepare for everything. I foolishly gambled on this one.

Doris and I arrived at the hospital the day before my morning operation. I was terrified, but only she knew it. The night before my surgery I was in my hospital bed when she looked at me the way she does when something is not quite right.

"OK," I said. "What's the problem?"

"You must tell the children," she said. "It's not right for you to have major surgery without saying something to them beforehand." I told her I did not want them to worry about me. I lost the argument.

I decided to tell them for her sake. I picked up the phone beside my hospital bed and called my son, Ian, at Harvard Medical School at that time. He was surprised by the news.

But Ian quickly analyzed my situation as calmly as if he were a member of my medical team. He promised to tell his siblings what was going on, adding he would send up a prayer for me.

The following morning was a blur. They hooked me up and knocked me out and I vaguely remember sweet dreams. When I awoke, I had no pain. None.

The catheter was uncomfortable and I had an upset stomach, but I was OK. The next day, the surgeon told me I would live a normal life and the nerve was saved. I remember speaking to my children soon afterward. I even conducted a conference call from my hospital bed regarding a possible contract in the Middle East. The ultimate test of my faith came the night before my surgery. It was as if I was having a final conversation with God:

Lord, You've given me a wonderful life. I am so grateful. If it's time for me to die, I'm ready. Amen.
Your nervous servant,
Wally

Chapter 15

U ntil recently, most Americans had never heard of the United Arab
Emirates, a federation of seven states located between Saudi Arabia and Oman on the Persian Gulf.

It was in 2006 when President George W. Bush backed a plan to give the UAE managerial control of six strategically important ports in the United States. Most Americans were not happy about it.

The deal eventually fell through, but six years prior to that, I knew precisely where the UAE was located. That little chunk of sand was Eagle Group International's springboard to the pinnacle of entrepreneurship.

The oil-rich Arab country was set to triple Eagle Group International's revenues to $22 million. After three years of negotiations, Eagle Group landed a fourteen-year agreement at $6 million per year initially and $10 million annually later. My team and I had worked the entire continental United States in search of contracts for Eagle Group. And when the big one finally came, it originated from an Arab country slightly smaller than Maine.

The United Arab Emirates needed help establishing, organizing, equipping and training its own military medical service. UAE representatives wanted to know which contractor could do the best job.

"We want to put our medics in good hands," the Arabs said. "Who do you recommend?"

We had already helped train U.S. Army medics and our reputation for integrity and efficiency was solid. While in the military, I had been in charge of modernizing our entire Army's medical services support. This, essentially, was what the UAE wanted for its military, so we got the job.

I had already become a millionaire by then. In celebration, Doris and I had a candlelight dinner at our home in South Carolina. That was it. We had more work to do. I don't get excited about business deals until the papers are signed and the first check clears the bank. I don't like disappointments.

I can't count the times people swore they would do business with me and nothing came of it. But the UAE contract was different. It was huge. It would make the Johnson family a heck of a lot more than "well off." And everything was looking good — for a while.

But trouble came, thanks to a North Carolinian whose own company would be the United Arab Emirates prime contractor for the project. In other words, this man technically was my boss. Eagle Group International was one of several subcontractors on the job. Initially, I could not have cared less who was coordinating the work.

During the three years it took to solidify the UAE deal, he had made scores of trips to the UAE to oversee contract negotiations. I never set foot in the country until the negotiations were completed and the contracts signed.

Whether you're dealing with the government of the United States or that of the United Arab Emirates, contract negotiations progress in a way that's universal – slowly. I knew Eagle Group was highly regarded by UAE officials. So I concentrated on other matters.

Many Americans mistakenly think the Middle East is a barren, unsophisticated land, and that people who live there are radically focused on their religion and on ways to spend their petroleum wealth. The folks I dealt with in the United Arab Emirates were not like that at all. They are intelligent and urbane. Several earned degrees from Oxford and Harvard universities. They spoke English better than most Americans.

The primary contractor finally closed the UAE contract in the year 2000 and I was ecstatic. Five years earlier, Doris and I were holding Eagle Group meetings around the kitchen table of our condo in Atlanta. Now we were part of one contract that would net us millions. I did not sleep for twenty-four hours after getting the call.

Doris and I soon flew out of Hartsfield International Airport in Atlanta for Abu Dhabi International Airport. After enjoying our meal aboard a Boeing 747, I finally fell sleep. I had done all my homework and was ready to impress everyone.

I awoke an hour or so before we were to land. As we approached Abu Dhabi, the capital of the United Arab Emirates, I looked out of the window at what appeared to be a spotless modern city full of skyscrapers. Abu Dhabi is a jewel smack dab in the middle of a desert that stretched as far as I could see.

A limousine was waiting for us at the airport. We soon checked into a hotel. It was early the next day when the limo returned to the front of the hotel and I got in. I was driven to the UAE's military headquarters.

I marveled at how polite everyone seemed to be. Abu Dhabi is a cosmopolitan city and very liberal compared to Muslim standards. The government is generally tolerant of other religions and consumption of alcohol is allowed in many bars and restaurants. I was a wide-eyed tourist and enjoyed it.

Oil was discovered in the UAE less than 50 years ago, so the buildings and roads are generally new and well constructed. The streets are full of Mercedes and other luxury automobiles from all over the world. I saw mansions bigger than the biggest ones in Beverley Hills. I grinned broadly as I took in everything.

Lord, help me to remember who I am, remind me where I came from. Help me to maintain balance and to hold true to those basic values that have brought me to this point. And of course, my good Jesus, thanks for getting me here.

A thankful servant,

Wally

Chapter 16

Once the ink dried on the United Arab Emirates agreement, it didn't take long for the lead contractor to demonstrate what he was all about. The UAE faithfully paid him in advance for the first quarter of the year 2000, but he only paid $1.3 million of the $2 million he owed us.

"Wally, my problem is that I'm just getting organized," he said convincingly. "My company is new and I'm trying to get my finance department squared away. Don't worry, I'll make it up to you."

I accepted his explanation. I too had started a company from scratch and understood his plight.

I was quite familiar with entrepreneurial growing pains, so I trusted him until we got his second-quarter check, which was short again. By then we were almost eight months into the UAE contract.

Meanwhile, the UAE military leaders expressed their appreciation for all Eagle Group had done for them thus far and let it be known that they wanted us to take on more responsibilities.

But individuals working for the primary contractor had different ideas. Instead of giving Eagle Group the additional work, they hired medical personnel to fulfill the request. It was obvious by then that Eagle Group was being cut out and they were keeping the change.

If the contract had been managed through the U.S. government, Eagle Group would be paid exactly what the agreement stipulated. It's the law. But the same rules did not apply in the UAE. Eagle Group International put virtually all its resources into the project. As a result of this 70 percent payment plan, Eagle Group International was several million dollars in debt by year's end.

In the spring of 2001, Eagle Group's prospects for remaining a viable business were grim. The prime contractor was paying us an ever-decreasing percentage of what he owed. I had a superb relationship with a former UAE military general officer who was my sponsor in his country, plus I knew the UAE medical bureaucrats who supervised the project. There was a strong and sincere desire within the UAE to see it through, so I figured at some point they would intervene on my behalf. As usual, on my daily walks I prayed the rosary and asked God for guidance.

But no one came through. Eagle Group International was owed more than $9 million when I returned to UAE in August 2001. According to provisions of the contract, they were informed that Eagle Group would not work on the contract after Sept. 29 because we did not get paid in full. What at first looked like a juicy plum had terribly soured. What was a renewable, fourteen-year contract would be terminated after only eighteen months. Unbelievable!

While I was in the UAE, rumors flew about the prime contractor and the debt his company was racking up among other subcontractors in addition to Eagle Group. I heard he owed numerous subcontractors that included some of the biggest corporations and most prestigious medical centers in the United States.

With each passing day, Eagle Group International moved closer to bankruptcy. How could this contract have turned out so badly?

I was determined to survive, but how I was going to do it was a mystery. Anyone who has run a successful business knows what I'm talking about. You often need to move from Point A to Point B with no map to show the way. I pride myself on being able to adapt to changing situations. Again, I turned to God, my ultimate business partner, and asked for help.

The road to my becoming a U.S. Army general officer was not straight, and it did not have convenient signposts along the way. I had to improvise. The U.S. military, contrary to one might think, is not all spit and polish. Its bureaucracy often forces people to get down and dirty in order to advance through the ranks.

So I relied on my hard-earned "street smarts" when devising a strategy for saving my company. I continued to communicate with my nemesis but our conversations did not result in his agreeing to pay what he owed.

We were not on the streets of Harlem or the sand lots in Charleston. We were in the Middle East. I knew I could not settle the matter the old-fashioned way. So I stopped fixating on the man and focused entirely on what was left of my company. We had other contracts to meet.

So there I was in Abu Dhabi on Sept. 11, 2001. I was walking past an Appleby's chain restaurant in the city when a man came out and pulled me inside to see the television screen. The Twin Towers on the south end of Manhattan Island had been destroyed. A section of the Pentagon, where I once worked, was a smoldering ruin. Another hijacked jumbo jet went down in a field in Pennsylvania.

Thousands of innocent Americans and others perished thanks to a Arab terrorists. The world had changed.

How could this have happened in the United States? Didn't we see it coming? Like most Americans, I felt a combination of rage, sadness and trepidation. As a retired Army officer, I was embarrassed.

I watched CNN recount the events back home. My UAE hosts were solicitous, but I couldn't help but wonder what the leaders of the UAE knew about the biggest terrorist assault that had ever occurred inside the United States of America. Was I a target?

With the help of friends in Abu Dhabi, I moved to what was considered a safe house but I continued to walk daily without fear. I knew my neighbors, so to speak.

A month later, I flew back to the United States feeling like I was en route to a funeral. America had entered a new era and I wasn't sure what would happen next. But I did know there would be hell to pay someday.

Divine Savior,

I ask that you give me the strength to clear this hurdle and courage to stay in the race. And God, help me keep my mind and heart open to the unexpected ways in which you always come to me.

Your Olympian-in-training,

Wally

Chapter 17

Getting my company refocused was the only thing on my mind when I sat down with Eagle Group International's top executives in January 2002. I had not even glanced at the agenda that morning when I rose from my chair slowly, looked each executive in the eyes for effect and said in a very low voice, "Let me tell you something."

I had their attention. They leaned forward so that they could hear what their normally gregarious boss was about to say.

"From this point forward, the initials U-A-E are off limits in my staff meetings. Here's why ..." I paused for effect.

"We have UAE-contract-on-the-brain around here. Our situation with that contract soured everyone's thinking and it has become a serious impediment, an obstacle. It's keeping us from embracing fresh perspectives and strategies that will allow this company to continue moving forward.

"So from this moment on, we will not talk about the UAE contract again during my staff meetings. "We're going to take all the energy that was devoted to that topic and we're going to re-direct it to discussions about how we can better serve our existing clients and bring in new ones. Is that clear?"

No one responded. But I know they got the message. My usual smile was absent.

"OK. Let's move on to the agenda," I said and sat down. I looked down at the agenda and the second item was "Discussion of the UAE Contract." I cleared my throat and added, "It goes without saying that we will not address No. 2 on the agenda this morning. Our goal is to be No. 1, not No. 2. So let's move on."

We rededicated ourselves that morning to making sure our clients were serviced properly and promptly and new ones would be found. I wrote a memorandum to that effect and posted it for everyone at Eagle Group International to see.

And it was energizing. Fixating on problems beyond one's control is a mistake. It is counterproductive and puts everyone on edge. It makes people feel powerless. It blunts performance. Judgment is clouded.

I was not going to let anyone steal my joy, so I went on with my life. And I expected everyone else on our team to do the same.

Good Lord,

I've never felt completely down and out because I remembered your words, "Come to me all you who labor and are heavily burdened, and I will refresh you."

Your optimistic entrepreneur,
Wally

Chapter 18

By the spring of the next year rumors were swirling that the UAE government wanted to settle the financial issues associated with our contract. I'd heard similar rumors before. In my mind, the UAE contract was a nightmare in which I would no longer participate.

But all the talk I was hearing got my undivided attention following a brief phone call from that prime contractor, with whom I continued to correspond.

"Hello, Wally," he said, "The UAE wants to talk."

"Uh?"

I did not know what to say. So I didn't.

But sure enough, I was soon contacted by the UAE embassy and asked to visit as soon as possible and discuss a settlement. So my son Terrell, who had become the vice president of Eagle Group International, and I drove from Atlanta to Washington D.C.

From there we took a cab to the UAE embassy, an imposing, alabaster-colored building at 3522 International Court N.W. We arrived confident with a well-reasoned plea to UAE's diplomatic corps that we hoped would spring loose some of the money we were owed.

The opulence inside the embassy was mind-boggling. Everything seemed to be gold-plated and shining. I was optimistic as we sat down for the conference.

I glanced over at my son, who remained expressionless. Seven of us sat around that wide, highly polished table and began talking like long-lost friends. I soon brought everything into focus.

"You know, we worked very hard for you and consistently produced quality work," I said as our hosts listened attentively. "But due to matters beyond my control, we have received only about 70 percent of what we are owed. I know that's not how the UAE conducts business, and I know you don't approve of our payment shortfall. Can we work something out?"

The UAE spokesman was a distinguished gentleman who wore wire-rimmed glasses. His hair was black and silky. He had a deep-chocolate complexion. He reminded me of professional golfer V.J. Singh. His suit was Western and expertly tailored. He looked as if he was at home in the United States of America. He spoke in a calm and thoughtful voice.

"Mr. Johnson. Your work is first-rate, always on time, and you have an excellent reputation. Eagle Group International is one of the top three U.S. companies with whom the UAE has done business."

Beaming, I glanced at Terrell, who remained expressionless.

"But having said that," the man continued, "please understand that we have paid the prime contractor in a timely manner, just as we pledged we would. We have given him all the money that we agreed to give at the start."

It felt like the air was being sucked out of the room as he spoke. Suddenly, I felt extremely naïve, but I had to respond intelligently. I took a deep breath.

All the anger and disappointment I carried with me for more than a year was about to detonate. After months of remembering the meek, trying to be humble, forgetting my pride, turning the other cheek and so on and so forth, I was going to get "personal," as they used to say in my old neighborhood.

I glanced over at Terrell again, then back at the others.

"Look," I said, "that prime contractor – you know who I'm talking about – has left me high and dry. He has five other companies to pay

91

besides Eagle Group, and all of them are huge international corporations.

"My company is family owned. A total of twenty-four of my relatives work for Eagle Group in one capacity or another. I'm talking about my wife and my children, my uncles and my aunts, and my cousins. If we don't get paid, we'll go broke! Do you understand?

"I will be disgraced. I will have failed for the first time in my life. I grew up in a tiny apartment in a public housing project. I graduated from high school, then from college. I joined the Army and worked my you-know-what off and became a brigadier general. I was a health-care coordinator in civilian life and then I founded my own company. All along I kept telling myself, 'I can do that!' And we were doing just fine until we hooked up with you guys. What's happening is not right and you know it."

The sweat beaded across my brow and dripped into my eyes. I always sweat when I get nervous.

I glanced again at Terrell and noticed he was shaking. He lowered his head to that shiny round table and I thought he was crying right there in that room full of proud male Arabs. So I started crying, too. I could not help it.

"No, General, no," the senior UAE official said.

I will never forget that moment. Everyone in that room was moved by a power impossible for me to describe. Pretense vanished. We were all just humans sitting there in that sparkling embassy building and simply trying to get along. The room was permeated by a distinct sense of brotherly love, the kind that the wisest prophets of all the great religions cite when they explained what really matters in this confounding world.

"We can make arrangements, Gen. Johnson," the spokesman of the delegation said. "We respect you and your family and the excellent job that all of you have done. So let's get this resolved."

I looked at him. I looked around the room at the others. I knew that

Eagle Group International would be paid and that we would survive. Terrell was sitting up tall by then and he was smiling.

When we left the room I mentioned to my son that I thought he was crying. He said, no. "I was mad, Dad, not sad," he whispered to me as we headed out the door, "about what that prime contractor had done to you."

Heavenly Father, keep me meek and humble no matter what. Help me to be thankful for the little things and I appreciate you giving me the ability to be an over-achiever alpha male with the sensitive touch.

Your tearful entrepreneur,
Wally

Chapter 19

The Arabs kept their word and paid an exceptionally generous amount of what Eagle Group International was owed. We were out of debt and the proverbial sea had parted. U.S. Defense Department-coordinated contracts were plentiful as the "War Against Terrorism" raged and we helped fight it. After losing our 8(a) status because Eagle Group had reached its revenue limit, we learned to compete successfully with the big corporations mainly because we had learned the ropes.

It was also at this time that corporate giant Lockheed Martin hired Eagle Group International to help upgrade the U.S. Centers for Disease Control, headquartered in Atlanta. Our workforce soared to 267 employees by the close of 2002, a 44 percent increase. I was 63 years old and getting tired. My sons A.J. and Terrell had taken over Eagle Group's daily operations and ran everything smoothly. I became what I call a "remote-control CEO." I could do most of what I needed to from home.

I slowly, almost imperceptibly, transferred my Eagle Group responsibilities to them, and they did not miss a beat. They were eager for more.

One day as I sat in my office at corporate headquarters, I looked out the window at our employee parking lot. It was full of cars. I marveled at how smoothly everything was going and how good God had been to me as an entrepreneur. I wept again, only this time it was tears of joy.

Doris and I talked quietly that evening, reminiscing about our forty-three years of marriage. She said she was ready for me to come home to stay.

Afterword

Retired Brigadier General Walter Johnson III says he's too old for resumé building so he now simply follows his heart in his adopted hometown of Georgetown, S.C.

"We have been given a lot," Johnson says, "and I'm fully aware of God's admonition that much is expected of me in return."

Johnson is working on several fronts, and is especially committed to AMI-KIDS-Georgetown. Johnson and businessmen Doc Lachicotte, of Pawleys Island, and Dick Rosen, of Myrtle Beach, and Lawly Pate Ford, a Pawleys Island civic leader, are raising $4 million to build a new campus on which to house troubled boys and girls who have been given a second chance to clean up their lives and stay out of trouble.

"Surveys of career criminals show that most of them got in trouble as teenagers and never managed to get out. But 81 percent of the young people who have been through AMI-KIDS did not re-enter the juvenile justice system. We believe we are two years away from having a million dollars in hand, then we'll ask various charitable foundations, corporations, philanthropists and others for the rest," he said.

Johnson also is working to build affordable housing in the city of Georgetown's West End, primarily an African-American community where he has purchased twenty lots for construction of modern and efficient homes.

"I don't like to use the term low-income housing because people tend to believe it's inferior housing," he said. "It is not inferior housing. It's for people who have low-income jobs. It's important that decent folks have decent homes."

Johnson said his decision to build the new houses was easy after visiting families living in trailers and shacks in the neighborhood. "I could see the ground through their floorboards and the stars through the holes in the roofs.

"I asked them why they didn't move out, and they said they didn't have anywhere else to go. We have already built one duplex and will complete five more soon. They are nice homes with central heat and air-conditioning as well as washing machines and dryers, and green space where children can play."

Johnson also serves as vice chairman of the Georgetown County Economic Development Commission and is a past chairman of the Georgetown County Chamber of Commerce. He serves on the Georgetown Health Systems board of directors, the Brookgreen Gardens board of trustees, the West Virginia State University Foundation board, the Horry-Georgetown Technical College Foundation board, the board of trustees for the Medical University of South Carolina Foundation and numerous other organizations. He is a principal in the Walter and Doris Johnson Charitable Foundation, and is a member of Sigma Pi Phi and Omega Psi Phi fraternities.

Dear God, Help me to be as successful in my desire to share your love and blessings with others as I have been in my military and post military careers. I promise in my retirement to be as tenacious, diligent and creative as ever in helping others be all they can be.

Your semi-retired servant,

Wally

Wally's Words to the Wise

● Learn to embrace setbacks. Most entrepreneurs will receive the sternest test of their resolve and management abilities during their first twelve months of operation. As painful as obstacles and pitfalls are, they help to strengthen managerial muscles never used before. Plus, if you resist letting aggravation and frustration cloud your vision, setbacks invariably open up marvelous new business opportunities. The trick is to determine what caused the setback in the first place and learn your lessons well.

● Out-hustling competitors and workers is key. Let's be honest – a key area where many small, minority-run businesses fall short is in the area of providing superior service. Always give your clients more than what they expect. And you, the owner, must set a good example. Strive to outwork everybody.

● Don't be afraid to be the dumbest person in the room. Along with being unable to manage money or people, few things will scuttle a new businessperson faster than pride. Hire the best and the brightest people that you can, and listen carefully to what they are saying.

● Low startup capital is a positive, not a negative. Many minority-owned businesses, especially African-American ones, start out with very little capital. Eagle Group International was no exception. But we learned quickly to be efficient and we were innovative. Identify your priorities early and focus in on what's important, not on what's easy.

- Always go worst-case scenario. When laying out a game plan or strategy, start out with the worst thing that could possibly happen, and what steps you would take to survive it. Other problems will seem easy in comparison.

- Honor thy employees. Treat your employees with respect and they will not let you down. Provide health insurance, vacations and other benefits. You will recoup these expenses with a dedicated workforce.

- There's no such thing as an 8 (a) slam dunk. I cringe when I hear people characterize government set-aside programs as guaranteed vehicles for success. The federal government's 8 (a) program for minority entrepreneurs is as competitive as anything else associated with free enterprise. Preparation and execution must not be taken for granted.

- Avoid making business your end-all and be-all. Running a company can kill you. Balance is key.

- Develop the ability to peer into the future (and around corners). Don't be shortsighted. Your business plan should be flexible but applicable for at least 18 months in advance.

- God is your ultimate business partner. Have confidence, plan carefully, work hard, maintain your integrity, strive to love others and pray often. God will help you if you ask.

Principles of Entrepreneurship

RELATIVE TO ONE'S SELF:

1. Have a strong faith in God.

2. Have initiative and be a self-starter, don't wait to be told.

3. Be self-confident and believe in yourself, even when people around you doubt your capabilities.

4. Know when to take prudent risks and demonstrate sound judgment; anybody can take chances.

5. Don't be afraid to be afraid, it can be a super motivator.

6. Be able to communicate your thoughts orally and in writing, others must understand where you are going and how you plan to get there.

7. Be able to perform under physical and mental stress or at least be able to deal with the negativism and naysayers.

8. Overcome obstacles or at least neutralize them and never let obstacles become show stoppers.

9. Be able to think outside the box.

10. Stay humble at all times, no matter how successful you are.

11. Set high standards and live by them.

12. Take care of your health, both mental and physical.

13. Surround yourself with intelligent people who are dedicated to your cause.

14. Develop good forecasting skills and ability to visualize the project's success.

RELATIVE TO ONE'S SELF AND ORGANIZATION:

15. Be almost obnoxious in setting goals and objectives and be just as obsessive in achieving them.

16. Be able to develop a plan and adjust as you execute your plan and be able to adapt to changing situations.

17. Know your leadership and management style and your leadership and management strengths and weaknesses and use them to your advantage.

18. Be the hardest worker in your organization thereby out-hustling everybody working around you.

19. Choosing sides/selecting the winning team: view the placement of personnel inserting round pegs in round holes.

20. Be loyal to subordinates first and place them as your personal top priority, and secondly, be just as loyal to others working with and around you.

21. Develop win-win situations in your personal relationships.

22. Correct problems but more importantly correct systems and don't get bogged down swatting gnats while elephants trample all over you and your organization.

23. Be an overachiever and be willing to go beyond the norm; strive to be number one and be tenacious about it and try to be first among the number ones.

24. Ensure your organization reflects your personal attributes and values.

Biography of Walter F. Johnson III

- Born August 13, 1939, in Charleston to Inez Middleton and Walter F. Johnson Jr. and reared in Charleston, S.C., as an only child.

- Attended Immaculate Conception pre-school, elementary school, middle school and high school, where he was a solid student and a star high school football and basketball player; co-captain of basketball team and selected the most valuable Immaculate Conception basketball player his senior year.

- Spent formative years in Gadsden-Green Projects (public housing), Charleston, S.C.

- Met wife Doris Ann Wright while she was in eighth grade at Avery Institute and he was a high school freshman; married Doris in 1959.

- As an eighth-grader, he began delivering the Evening Post, the Charleston afternoon paper, and won second place in a city-wide contest for gaining the most new subscribers; later changed to morning paper route, and after some time, his supervisor combined two routes giving him the largest in entire city.

- Took saxophone lessons and later played in the West Virginia State College Marching and Touring Bands.

- Attended West Virginia State College from 1957 to 1961; graduated with a Bachelor of Science degree in zoology and minor in botany. Completed four years of Army Reserve Officer Training Corps studies. While at West Virginia State, he was a member of ROTC, student council, Omega Psi Phi Fraternity, Pan Hellenic Council, Newman Club (President of Catholic club for three years), Band, French Club, Academy of Science, and other organizations.

- First son, Walter F. Johnson IV, born in 1959 in Charleston, S.C.

- RoxAnne F. Johnson, first daughter, born in 1960 in Columbia, S.C.

- Entered active military service as second lieutenant in July 1961 in the

Medical Service Corps, U.S. Army in San Antonio, Texas.

● Assigned to Fort Bragg as medical platoon leader in the 504th Battle Group, 82nd Airborne Division.

● Second daughter, Rhoda A. Johnson, born in 1962 at Fort Bragg, N.C.

● Promoted to first lieutenant in January 1963.

● In July 1963, he was transferred to 8th Medical Battalion, 8th Infantry Division, Mainz, Germany.

● Second son, Terrell F. Johnson, born in 1963 in Wiesbaden, Germany.

● Held various jobs in 8th Medical Battalion between 1963 and 1966, received several commendations and recognitions to include the Army Commendation Medal for outstanding service.

● Promoted to captain in April 1964.

● Reassigned to Medical Field Service School, Fort Sam Houston, Texas; graduated from Officer Career Course in December 1966.

● Transferred to 44th Medical Brigade, Saigon, Vietnam; worked as plans and force structure officer concurrently for both the 44th Medical Brigade and 1st Logistics Command from January 1967 to January 1968, received Bronze Star for Outstanding service.

● Returned to Fort Sam Houston, Texas, to teach at the Medical Field Service School from January 1968 to May 1970; promoted to major; received Meritorious Service Medal for exceptionally outstanding service.

● Third son, A. Jason Johnson, born in March 1969 at Fort Sam Houston, San Antonio, Texas.

● Attended Command and General Staff College from July 1970 to May 1971; graduated; because he was in top five percent of class during first semester, he was selected to attend civilian graduate school.

● Fourth son, Ian T. Johnson, born at Fort Leavenworth, Kansas.

● Attended University of Missouri at Kansas City from 1971 to 1972, graduated with masters of science in International Relations.

● Assigned to United States Army's Office of the Surgeon General,

Washington, D.C., in July 1972, held several operational and planning positions to include chief of the Force Structure Branch; received the U.S. Army Meritorious Service Medal for exceptionally outstanding service upon reassignment in May 1977.

- Promoted to lieutenant colonel in July 1976.
- Transferred to 2nd Medical Battalion, 2nd Infantry Division, Camp Casey, Korea, where he commanded the 8th Medical Battalion from May 1977 to May 1978; received cluster (2nd award), the Meritorious Service for exceptionally outstanding service.
- Returned to the Office of the Surgeon General in 1978, held position of Assistant Executive Officer (assistant chief of staff to the Army Surgeon General).
- Attended the Industrial College of the Armed Services in Washington, DC from 1980 to 1981, graduated.
- Assigned to OTSG as Assistant Chief of the Medical Service Corps and concurrently Deputy Director of Personnel.
- Promoted to colonel in 1981.
- Promoted to the Executive Officer position (chief of staff) of OTSG. Selected Chief of the Medical Service Corps in 1985; concurrently, held the positions of Executive Officer (Chief of Staff) and Chief of the Medical Service; received second award of the U.S. Army Legion of Merit Medal.
- Promoted to brigadier general and commanded 5,000 officers in the Medical Service Corps; concurrently held the positions of director of U.S. Army worldwide health-services operations and chief of the Medical Service Corps; received the Distinguished Service Medal, the Army's highest award for achievement, in all positions; first African American in these positions, youngest officer to hold these positions; and took special courses at Harvard's John F. Kennedy School of Government.
- Inducted into the West Virginia State College Reserve Officer Training

Corps Hall of Fame in 1985.

● Inducted into the International Circulation Managers Association Newspaper Carrier Hall of Fame, which included the Golden Medallion Award in 1986.

● Upon retirement in September 1988, became director of Region 7 of the American Hospital Association, Dallas, Texas; received the American Hospital Association Service Leader Award for exceptionally outstanding service.

● Became senior vice president, American Hospital Association, in September 1990.

● Became president of the Institute for Diversity in Health-Services Management in June 1993, organized the foundation and was its first president and CEO.

● Formed Eagle Group International, Incorporated in March 1996; Within 12 years the family grew the company from zero to over $150 million in revenue; family sold Eagle Group to Lockheed Martin Corporation in 2008.

● Boards and organizations: past chairman of AMI/KIDS-Georgetown and now serves on executive committee; vice chairman Georgetown Economic Commission; member Georgetown Hospital System; member (Waccamaw Community Hospital; member, Brookgreen Gardens Board of Trustees; Thesauristes of Sigma Pi Phi Fraternity; member Omega Psi Phi Fraternity; member West Virginia State University Foundation; past chairman, Georgetown Chamber of Commerce; senior advisor, Georgetown Boys Mentor Group; member of 100 BLACK Men of America. Former member of Butler Street YMCA, Atlanta, GA; member, Teach MY People; advisor at St. James Santee Health Center; member of the National Association of Health Care Executives, co-vice chairman of the Clara Barton Society, Georgetown County Red Cross.